John G. Whittier

American Men of Letters

JOHN GREENLEAF WHITTIER

BY

GEORGE RICE CARPENTER

BOSTON AND NEW YORK

HOUGHTON, MIFFLIN AND COMPANY

The Riverside Press, Cambridge

1906

" *Dille: Madonna, lo suo core è stato*
  Con sì fermata fede,
  Ch' a voi servir lo pronta ogni pensiero:
  Tosto fu vostro, e mai non s' è smagato."

PREFACE

THE printed sources for the life of Whittier are
the volumes of William S. Kennedy (1881 and
1892); of Francis H. Underwood (1883), written with Whittier's consent and in part with his
help; the authorized biography by Samuel T.
Pickard (1894), which contains virtually all the
matter included in the earlier volumes as well as
much fresh material; and the little books of
reminiscences by Mrs. Mary B. Claflin (1893)
and Mrs. James T. Fields (1893). I am deeply
indebted to all these sources; to the admirable
biography of William Lloyd Garrison, prepared
by his children; to Mr. Pickard, who kindly allowed me to examine his collection of such of
Whittier's early verses as have not been republished; to Whittier's cousins, the Misses Johnson and Mrs. Woodman, who furnished me with
much new material; to Mr. Charles Francis
Adams, who sent me copies of Whittier's letters to John Quincy Adams; to Mr. William H.
Hayne, who sent me copies of Whittier's letters
to his father, Paul Hamilton Hayne; to Judge

Cowley, of Lowell, Mass., who found for me the
unique file of the " Middlesex Standard ; " and
to many other kind friends and correspondents
who have patiently borne my many questionings.

From the mass of new and old material I have
done my best to reconstruct the essential Whittier — the heritage, the environment, the temperament, the motives that constituted him and
none other ; and I think I have been at least successful in determining, to an extent not before
attained, the course of evolution of his literary
art. If I am wrong in any of my generaliza-
tions, the fault will, I hope, be in some measure
due to the comparative incompleteness of the
material. Whittier was modest and reticent, carrying these virtues almost to an extreme ; but it
would be strange if there did not somewhere
exist very considerable bodies of letters and
reminiscences that would aid us in tracing further the development of his genius. On whoever
holds any such precious and perishable material,
whether in the form of written documents, of
direct memories, or of oral tradition, I beg to
urge the imperative duty of having it at once
examined, and of taking proper measures to
secure its use and preservation.

G. R. C.

September, 1903.

CONTENTS

CHAP.   PAGE

   I. BOYHOOD, 1807–1828 1

  II. BOYHOOD, 1821–1828 25

 III. THE YOUNG JOURNALIST AND POLITICIAN,
       1829–1832 53

  IV. THE YOUNG ABOLITIONIST, 1833–1840 . 103

   V. REFORMER AND MAN OF LETTERS, 1840–
       1860 174

  VI. POET, 1860–1892 255

APPENDIX

   I. WHITTIER'S AUTOBIOGRAPHICAL LETTER . 297

  II. LIST OF WHITTIER'S WRITINGS . . . 304

INDEX 309

The portrait which forms the frontispiece to this volume is from an ambrotype taken about 1857, in the possession of Mr. Samuel T. Pickard.

JOHN GREENLEAF WHITTIER

CHAPTER I

BOYHOOD

1807–1828

JOHN GREENLEAF WHITTIER, journalist, politician, reformer, and poet, was born December 17, 1807, in the east parish of Haverhill, in Essex County, Massachusetts. In the early nineteenth century, New England, that part of the land in which intellectual and spiritual life among the common people had been most continuous and vigorous, was thoroughly fertilized, as it were, by generations of mental activity, and was ready to bear the natural fruit of the vitalized soil, — the man of letters, the man who fashions, in visible speech and in the mysterious forms of the imagination, the latent ideals and aspirations of his dumb fellows. And men of letters sprang up in abundance, great and small, in all the territory of these ancient colonies, and especially in the eldest, Massachusetts, from the almost solitary Bryant at the western border to the

larger company of the older eastern counties.
Of these eastern counties none was more fertile in this rare but inevitable human product
than Essex, where Whittier and Hawthorne were
born and lived.

The members of this New England band were
variously endowed, and were in many fashions
typical of the thought and life of their kin, of
their neighbors, of their native towns, counties,
and states, and to some extent of the country
at large. Of them all Whittier was the most
widely and profoundly and permanently representative of the common people of his locality.
His family had lived in that county since 1638,
on that farm since 1647, in that house since
1688, and only a few years of his long life were
spent outside of that district. No essential con-
stituent of his physical or intellectual nature
separated him from the great mass of his fellows. In his boyhood he toiled with his hands,
he read by the fireside, he drew his slender
formal education from the district school and the
town academy. His habits, his circumstances,
and all his interests bound him to the land and
the life of the people. Bryant early withdrew
himself from his simple native surroundings to
the complex environment of a large mercantile
city. Emerson came of a long line of men specially educated and set apart for a learned pro-

fession : it was natural that he should be a pioneer in thought, the prophet who led the people
from afar. Longfellow and Lowell were men
of a college community, fed on the new learning
of Europe ; Holmes was a man of a special city
and a special caste,— circumstances which largely
isolated and localized his sympathies and his
tastes ; Hawthorne, though he was born of an
old, permanently localized stock, and lived in a
small city, was so widely different from his fellows, so distinctly solitary, as not to be immediately representative of them. Whittier alone
was country born and country bred, a country
man in education and sympathies : a Haverhill
boy, an Amesbury man, he never broke the
slightest of the ties that bound him to his family
and his neighbors. His power of expression
was his own, but his life and his thoughts were
as theirs, and he thus became directly typical of
his town and his district, and indirectly typical
of all the country folk of his race and his nation
who lived the same simple life, based on the old
polity of the Puritan community. In the biography of such a man, unique among the greater
New England men of letters, we shall not find
ourselves concerned with any highly specialized
social or professional group of American writers,
or with native intelligence as modified by foreign travel and by the influence of European

philosophy or letters, but rather with the undiverted development of a peculiarly native writer, under the stimulus only of his natural environment and of the great local or national forces to which he and the mass of his fellows were subjected.

The tale of Whittier's ancestry is not long or rich in details. Like Burns, like Carlyle, like Defoe, he sprang directly from a long line of laboring men, without the intermediate generation or more of sedentary life which brought such different influences to bear on Bryant, Longfellow, and Lowell. The emigrant Whittier, Thomas, was perhaps a Huguenot, though there is little ground for thinking that his family was recently of French extraction, for the English surname — pronounced Whicher, as is the name of a hill in Amesbury which lay in the old Whittier grant — may be traced back to a considerably older period. Thomas was apparently an ideal pioneer. He came to the new land as a lad of eighteen; he was of great size and power; he married young and had many children; he played an honest and manly part in those troublous times, when energy of body and simplicity and sincerity of mind were of more value to the community than riches or learning. It was in 1638 that he came to New England, with his uncles, John and Henry Rolfe, — the latter of whom willed him the hive of bees which the early records carefully specify,— and a distant relative, Ruth Green, whom he married shortly afterward. He first settled in Salisbury near the Powow River, whose falls were to turn the mills of Amesbury, and was representative of that town in the General Court. He soon moved across the Merrimac to Newbury, the mother town of that district, and then in 1647 back again to the northern side of the beautiful river, this time to the young town of Haverhill. Here he was allotted land,— probably containing some of the natural meadow land, precious to the old settlers,— on the road from Salisbury that he had helped to lay out, and on the banks of Country Brook, some four or five miles from the little frontier settlement, from which it was separated by a range of broad-backed hills. He built him a log house, and threw himself into the long task, not to be completed for several generations, of clearing the wilderness and cultivating the rocky but fertile soil. He had ten children, of whom five were boys, each over six feet in height. His name occurs from time to time in the town records, and he was apparently a man to be trusted and depended on. He was one of a committee to determine the bounds of the plantation, and as an outlying settler he helped in determining and establishing the various garrison houses, in

which the isolated might find nightly shelter
when there was danger of attack by Indians.
But it is related that he and his family, secure
in their integrity, did not avail themselves of the
protection of a fortified house not far distant,
and though often visited by savages, were never
harmed.[1]   The only censure associated with the
pioneer was one that now serves as a source of
praise.   In 1652 complaint was made against
Joseph Peasley and Thomas Macy, of the part
of Salisbury in which Whittier had first settled
and of which he was now not a distant neighbor,
for exhorting people on the Sabbath in the absence of the minister, and a law was passed re-
straining them from this evil practice.   This
was in the very earliest days of the Quakers,
before their missionaries had come to New England ; and though both men afterwards became
Quakers, there is no ground for believing that
there was then aught against them save that terrible jealousy of the priesthood, unhappy cause
of many evils, against whatever seemed to break
down its privileges.   At all events the brave
Robert Pike, one of the noblest men of the district, openly declared the act to be one contrary
to the liberties of the country, both civil and

[1] The terrible Indian raids to which the little frontier village was exposed are well described by Whittier in his " Boy
Captives," *Prose Works*, ii. 395.

ecclesiastical. He was therefore disfranchised, disabled from holding any public office, bound to good behavior, and fined twenty marks. This unjust sentence caused a great sensation in the neighboring towns, and many petitions were sent to the General Court in his behalf, including one from Haverhill, signed by Whittier. The inexorable and priest-ridden lawgivers made some show of punishing even the petitioners, and it is said that Whittier was deprived of his franchise, which was restored only in 1666.

About 1688, at the age of sixty-eight, Thomas Whittier built himself a second and more substantial house, half a mile or so from the first, and still on the road from Haverhill to Salisbury, in a wooded fold of the hulking hill that shuts off that part of the town from Haverhill. In 1696, when the old man died, the children had apparently scattered to homes of their own, after the fashion that has built up our land so rapidly, save the youngest son, Joseph, who, following another old custom, remained on the farm. He was born in 1669, and in 1694 he had married Mary Peasley, daughter of Joseph Peasley, whose fine old homestead, built of bricks brought over from England, still stands a few miles away by the riverside. Mary's grandfather was the unlicensed exhorter whose rights the elder Whittier had upheld, and who had afterwards become a member of the Society of Friends. The bitter persecutions of the Quakers by the tyrannical clergy had by this time been stopped by the application of sound English law, but they were still a people set apart and not yet free from suspicion, and Joseph's marriage to a Quakeress is evidence that he was sufficiently liberal to adopt her faith.

The youngest son of Joseph's nine children, likewise a Joseph,[1] was born in 1716, married Sarah Greenleaf of the neighboring town of West Newbury in 1739, and, like his father before him, stayed by the homestead. The youngest sons of eleven children were John and Moses, who at his death bought the interest of the other heirs in the estate and remained on the farm. John was born in 1760. At the age of forty-

---

[1] In "The Great Ipswich Fright" (*Prose Works*, ii. 385) Whittier gives a pleasant anecdote of the imperturbability of this old Quaker.

"All through that memorable night the terror swept onward towards the north with a speed which seems almost miraculous, producing everywhere the same results. At midnight a horseman, clad only in shirt and breeches, dashed by our grandfather's door, in Haverhill, twenty miles up the river. 'Turn out! Get a musket! Turn out!' he shouted; 'the regulars are landing on Plum Island!' 'I 'm glad of it,' responded the old gentleman from his chamber window; 'I wish they were all there, and obliged to stay there.' When it is understood that Plum Island is little more than a naked sandridge, the benevolence of this wish can be readily appreciated."

four he married Abigail Hussey, twenty-one years younger than himself. Their four children were, Mary, born in 1806; John Greenleaf, born in 1807; Matthew Franklin, born in 1812; and Elizabeth Hussey, born in 1815.

Such were the links of life that bound Whittier to the soil,— a great-great-grandfather, a giant pioneer, who hewed out a homestead in the wilderness; a great-grandfather, a grandfather, and a father, all younger sons, who each married a farmer's daughter and kept the homestead in his turn. We know little of what they did, nothing of what they said and thought; it was a silent ancestry, a typical New England ancestry of toil and independence and content. Indeed, in the case of his immediate parents, the record is not much fuller. His father had married late; was a prompt, decisive man; had in his earlier days been to and fro between Essex County and Canada for common barter; was, like his forefathers, a trustworthy man and just, holding minor town offices with approval, respected in his religious society. An old man when his sons were lads, he had learned the farmer's wisdom that overrules the rash impulses of youth and shuts out vain fancies, and he warned his boys against the folly of trying to be aught but what the generations before him had been. It was the mother,— far younger than her husband,— from whom Whittier and his sister Elizabeth drew their brilliant eyes and emotional sensitiveness,[1] who understood best the son and cherished his ambitions. She was a beautiful and godly woman, full of a saintly peace and an overflowing human kindness which made her a very type of her religion.

Such were the qualities that were Whittier's physical heritage or early presented for his imitation. They were in the main conservative influences, such as would attach him to the seventeenth century homestead, so well founded and so well protected. Physically, it was a robust heritage, for was he not the son of an active and resolute farmer, of a race of sturdy pioneers, save that, perhaps, as a late-born son of a line of younger sons, his was a more delicate and less powerful frame, of the nervous type that wears long but must labor less unremittingly. Intellectually, it was a sincere and trustworthy heritage. He would have been false to all tradition, had he, with such a past, been a careless citizen, a faithless friend, or an unworthy man. In all respects it was a typical New England

[1] It is usually said that the mother was a descendant of Stephen Bachiler, the famous old Portsmouth preacher, whose striking appearance was transmitted to many of his posterity, among them both Whittier and Webster. But the genealogy in Whittier's case has been proved false. See *N. E. Historical and Genealogical Register*, 1896, i. 295.

heritage, and his birth had seemingly given him neither more nor less than the common lot of his fellows.

We may now look with more definiteness to the surroundings of his earlier years, which moulded the young spirit before it had grown strong enough to have its own individuality, while he was still highly receptive, without personal choice, of the influences acting upon him.

In later life, replying to questions as to his early life, Whittier said : —

" I think at the age of which thy note inquires I found about equal satisfaction in an old rural home, with the shifting panorama of the seasons, in reading the few books within my reach, and dreaming of something wonderful and grand somewhere in the future. Neither change nor loss had then made me realize the uncertainty of all earthly things. I felt secure of my mother's love, and dreamed of losing nothing and gaining much. . . . I had at that time a great thirst for knowledge and little means to gratify it. The beauty of outward nature early impressed me, and the moral and spiritual beauty of the holy lives I read of in the Bible and other good books also affected me with a sense of my falling short and longing for a better state." [1]

[1] Pickard, *Life*, i. 26.

The region in which Whittier spent his life is singularly charming and, it may be added, very typical of New England.   Remote from the life of a large city,— so properly stimulating to the mature, so improperly stimulating to the young, — the district was yet near enough to a port of considerable importance to make a child sensible of the outer world and its currents of trade.   It presented an admirable diversity of prospect. Within sight of the mountains, within sound of the sea, it had its forests and intervales, its rounded glacial hills, its marshes and meadow land and orchards and planted fields, its beautiful lakes and its noble river.   Besides these outward charms the district had to the reflective mind another attraction : it was his.   His ancestors had lived there since first the wilderness path was trodden by white men ; it had a wealth of impressive local legend and history ; and none of all this associative influence was lost on the lad.   Many of his poems stick so closely to the familiar landscape that only the native can take in their full meaning, and the stranger must read them map in hand ; and his prose sketches look back to the old scenes.   In them he recalls more specifically than in his verse the scenes impressed so deeply on his early recollections : —

"The old farmhouse nestling in its valley ; hills stretching off to the south and green meadows to the east; the small stream which came noisily down its ravine, washing the old garden-wall and softly lapping on fallen stones and mossy roots of beeches and hemlocks; the tall sentinel poplars at the gateway; the oak forest, sweeping unbroken to the northern horizon; the grass-grown carriage-path, with its rude and crazy bridge,— the dear old landscape of my boyhood lies outstretched before me like a daguerreotype from that picture within, which I have borne with me in all my wanderings." [1]

"Our old homestead (the house was very old for a new country, having been built about the time that the Prince of Orange drove out James the Second) nestled under a long range of hills which stretched off to the west. It was sur-rounded by woods in all directions save to the southeast, where a break in the leafy wall re-vealed a vista of low green meadows, picturesque with wooded islands and jutting capes of upland. Through these a small brook, noisy enough as it foamed, rippled, and laughed down its rocky falls by our garden-side, wound, silently and scarcely visible, to a still larger stream, known as the Country Brook. This brook in its turn, after doing duty at two or three saw and grist mills, the clack of which we could hear in still days across the intervening woodlands, found its

[1] "Yankee Gypsies," in *Prose Works*, i. 330.

way to the great river, and the river took up and bore it down to the great sea." [1]

The house of the Whittiers was of the older, the pioneer type. Thousands like it exist in New England, though few are so excellently preserved, and none is so deservedly famous, for this single dwelling has become in literature the type of all the homely houses in which New England families gathered around their firesides in the days now gone, in a fashion of life now almost entirely passed away in that section of the country. This homestead, which Whittier himself described in " Snow-Bound," was of a type wholly conformable to the needs and spirit of country life, as different as could be from the mansions of the South or even from those of Boston and Newburyport. Those were for the gentry, that small class that loomed for a while so large in American history, played so well its part, and finally became virtually extinct as its policy became more falsely conservative, more essentially un-American, less sensitive to the great principles of honor and justice and equality. The stately buildings of Beacon Street meant less for the commonwealth than the homesteads of Essex County, whose simple structure followed

---

[1] " The Fish I Did n't Catch," in *Prose Works*, i. 320. See also " My Summer with Dr. Singletary," *ibid.*, in which the neighboring district by the riverside, the " Rocks," is described in detail.

the needs of a household in which servants were
unknown; the company that gathered around
the hearth was united in mutual dependence, —
a dependence typical of the relations of all citizens to one another and to the state.

The kin and the guests that met in the great-
chimneyed kitchen were equally typical of New
England. Of the father and the mother we
have already spoken. There were also brothers
and sisters, each quiet or gay, practical or
dreamy, according to his temperament; a
maiden aunt, who might have had her own
household had the lover lived whose apparition
so strangely visited her at the hour of his death
in a distant place; and a bachelor uncle, one
of the sort found in every New England village,
but scarcely known in literature except through
the personality of Thoreau, — an unworldly
man, fond of the woods and fields and their
denizens, a faint and less strenuous survival of
the pioneer. Of guests there were the winter
schoolmasters, country lads themselves, adding
to the slender resources needed for their education by teaching in the college vacation, pur-
posely lengthened for such as they, — striplings
themselves, but stimulating boys to acquire
learning, and destined almost invariably to play
well their diverse parts in later life. There
came, too, the pedler with his pack and his

gossip; the visiting Friend, sometimes a man of renown, for the yearly meeting at Amesbury was well attended; the companionable neighbor; the chance traveller, hung about with the glamour of foreign lands, and bringing to a spot apparently so isolated the sense of the huge outer world, as the eastern winds brought sometimes to the hill farm the thunder of the Atlantic surf. Such companionship and such influences were indeed rural, rustic, but these words must not be applied in any contemptuous sense. A group like this was ignorant of city ways, but it possessed in itself all the elements — save, perhaps, knavery — which, variously combined, constitute the interests, the ambitions, the toil, and the weariness of life. Quietly the country boy could learn his great lesson.

With this ancestry, in this environment, Whittier spent his boyhood in the placid labor and simple sport of the farmer's lad. Physically the life was in many respects ill suited to a delicate constitution. Thoughtlessly subservient in such matters to tradition, the farmers dried their fresh meat by excessive cooking, ate too much salt food, clothed themselves too thinly, ignored too openly the now plain hygiene of life, and weaklings fell an easy prey to consumption or survived to live the death-in-life of the dyspeptic. But even on the physical side there were compensations, and in the city almost the same evils existed, in an epoch of lanky sallowness that is only now passing away from the nation as a whole. The life in the open air, the diversity of labor and its many intermissions, the companionship with animals, the freedom from hurry and irritation, were good for boy and man, and Whittier clung long to the farming life, and never spoke of it contemptuously, knowing what was the mingled joy and torture of slowly wringing, by the sweat of the brow, the necessaries of life from a not too fertile soil. And on the intellectual and spiritual side, there was much to be gained. Less learned in books than Longfellow or Holmes or Lowell, he had perforce a stronger hold in boyhood on certain excellent elements of character, — industry, frugality, patience, and independence.

We may now pause a moment, before taking up the actual narrative of Whittier's boyhood, to see if we can determine the fundamental principles of life, if such they may be called, which he unconsciously absorbed from his early environment and which were later to be strongly effective in determining his course of action.

It is plain that we cannot be wrong, in the first place, in throwing stress upon a principle of local permanency, a feeling of attachment to a given locality. Father and son, the Whittiers had been for centuries associated with a special place and owned brotherhood to the men of the district, to whom they were allied by relationship, by common interests, by long association, and by similar habits of speech, thought, and action. They were Essex County men, — more specially still, Haverhill men, — and they formed a clan of their own, a clan based less on actual kinship than on permanent connection with a given spot, on citizenship in a given district. Other districts there were within the boundaries of the state and the group of related states. Each, too, had its particular characteristics and associations. And so to Whittier's young eyes New England must have seemed a great series of commonwealths within commonwealths, each with its particular identity well preserved, — a state of mind not easily clear to the metropolitan boy of to-day, whose stock has usually been several times transplanted, and who in his nomadic existence has acquired small allegiance to any spot of soil or group of men. One has only to read " Massachusetts to Virginia " or the boyish "Song of the Vermonters," to understand how clearly Whittier visualized and localized the kindred clans and tribes of New England.

A second basis of thought and action familiar to Whittier was that of local independence. Each of the districts we have described was, to

a very considerable extent, not only politically
but intellectually, spiritually, and socially independent. It had its own schools, which sufficed
it, its own newspapers, its own churches, subject to no outside interference and needing no
outside help, its own circles of friends and
neighbors, into which strangers rarely entered.
Haverhill, Merrimac, and Amesbury all turned
to Newburyport as a large trading centre and
port of entry, but with no feeling of suburban-
ness. Boston was a distant city, the recent seat
of the General Court, and a place of size and
importance, but it had apparently no more influence on Whittier's boyhood than London. It
was scarcely forty miles from Newburyport, but
he seems to have visited it only once before
he was twenty. The urban movement had not
yet begun, and the placid villages dwelt serenely
apart, like Homer's Cyclopes, makers of their
own fates.

Thirdly, the New England villager felt in his
heart of hearts that if he deliberately set for
himself a goal of ambition, and was willing to
bend himself to it with enthusiasm, he could
count, humanly speaking, on attaining it. No
career was closed to the man of intelligence and
industry. The country was growing rapidly,
and her needs outran her supply of men. She
could use all her own worthy sons and all that

came from abroad. There was, comparatively speaking, little competition, and intellectual life of all sorts was so young, so far from complex, that one could scarcely move a step without opening up vistas of the unknown, waiting to be appropriated by some stalwart brain that could, like the pioneer, subdue the tangle of the wilderness. Country birth or a slender education was no bar to success. High aspirations and persistent industry were the essentials, and we find both Whittier and Garrison, born of families in which the men lived by manual labor, with little education and only a modicum of special training, declaring that they would yet make the land ring with their fame, quite as confidently as did the young Longfellow, whose ancestors had for four generations been men of education, and who was at almost precisely the same time giving expression to a similar desire for glory.

Last of all, a strong religious element was very frequently present in the young New Englander of the time. The outward hold of the rigid old orthodoxy was slowly weakening, especially throughout eastern Massachusetts; Unitarian and Universalist churches were springing up, and there was a growing tendency to accept whatever forms of religious thought showed more affection toward God and more tenderness toward man. The power of the clergy, still jeal-

ously defended, was a mere shadow of its former
self and was destined soon to be broken entirely.
But this outward decay of a formal creed was
merely a sign that the essentials of the faith it
so clumsily expressed were being thoroughly absorbed by the people at large. The active principle of Puritanism had done its work. This
great movement had been begun to insist on the
purification of the church, to restore the pristine
faith of Christ in its purity. The established
churches resisted the movement; as permanent
organizations they claimed the right to determine the faith, to set the creed. The new tenet
of the Puritans, the tenet that colonized the
Western world, was that the faith had already
been determined by its founder, and was specifically defined, not by a self-perpetuating organization, but by a written contract or constitution,
the Scriptures; from the theory of salvation
as there laid down the established churches had
obviously departed. In these propositions they
were clearly logically correct. Granted the va-
lidity of the Scriptures as a complete revelation,
it was plain that all intelligent minds could act
upon their prescriptions, and could thus have
access to the source of the law. The influence
of this deduction was enormous. In the midst
of the mad attempt to rule communities of the
seventeenth century in accordance with the in-

tricate and contradictory records of the early
tribal legislation of the Hebrews, one main doctrine retained its efficacy,— the doctrine that the
people interpret the law of God,— and this combined with the passion for political independence, of which it was in part the cause, to give
the New England Puritan both a desire that
God's will should be done and a conviction that
he could himself determine what God's will was
likely to be.

Not only was Whittier reared in this general
atmosphere of Puritanism, with its emphasis on
the democratic interpretation of the Scriptures
and its passion for justice, but he was more particularly influenced by the doctrines of the Society of Friends. The Quakers were the ultra-
Puritans of the seventeenth century. They would
have revivified all the inherent democratic and
individualistic principles of the Gospels. They
would call no man master, nor show more respect to one than to another. They lived simply
and spoke plainly. They cultivated mercy and
loving-kindness. Could Christ have come to
earth again, they it would clearly have been, of
all the Western followers of an Oriental creed,
that He would have recognized as most patiently
following out the tenets He had laid most
stress on.

But the essential difference between the Qua-

kers and the other forms of revolt against the
established and organized churches lay in the
stress that they laid upon the rights of the individual and his access to the source of authority.
To them the written word of God was not all
sufficient. The soul of the believer was open to
the promptings of the spirit ; the inner light, the
voice of God, would lead him. Such a principle
opened the way for idiosyncrasies and whimsi-
calities on the part of individuals, but, controlled
by the judgment of the whole community of be-
lievers, it led to little evil and brought about
much good. It constantly tended to weaken the
force of convention, to strengthen the conscience,
to open the mind to new conceptions of justice,
and to inculcate essential honesty and righteousness as distinguished from the code of morals
prescribed by a definite creed. Much has been
said of the rise of Unitarianism in New England
as marking the breaking down of the rigid religious conceptions of the eighteenth century and
the awakening of new moral forces that acted
powerfully for advancement in civilization. But
the Unitarian movement, in most respects, merely
meant that educated people, showing the effects
of generations of cultivation, were reaching a
conception of life that the simple-minded Quakers had long before made their own. It seems
to be a law of life that moral advancement is

not primarily the work of the wise but of the ignorant, of babes and sucklings.

In brief, then, we may see that in spiritual and religious matters Whittier was deeply influenced by principles that were ultra-Puritan, logically Puritan, but far in advance of the common orthodoxy of his day, and was thus typical not only of the current religious belief in New England but of the great impulse toward reform that lay dormant therein.

CHAPTER II

1821–1828

WHITTIER'S lot was that of the farmer's boy.
He was brought up to take his share in the tasks
of the family. "At an early age," he said, in
the autobiographical leaflet with which in later
life he used to answer inquiries about his boyhood,[1] " I was set at work on the farm, and doing errands for my mother, who, in addition to
her ordinary house duties, was busy in spinning
and weaving the linen and woollen cloth needed
in the family." Later there came, as his strength
allowed, the lighter tasks of the barn and the
field, and then the more taxing. All this was
excellent training for body and mind, — better
indeed for the mind than for the body. Intellectual habits may sometimes be best acquired
through manual labor. Whittier's neatness and
accuracy of mind, the cool judgment and readi-
ness of intelligence which he displayed from the
very outset of his studies, probably had much to
do with the discipline he received from his work

[1] Reprinted in Appendix, i.

on the farm. But if his intellect grew, his
body suffered. Ambition or necessity led him
to forms of labor too severe for his strength,
and the swinging of the flail left him with dis-
abilities that lasted through his life; the exposure with insufficient clothing to the bitter
New England weather gave him a bronchial
weakness; and the bad food caused dyspepsia.
If all the possibilities of his great career came
from the opportunities offered by his ancestry
and his environment, all the bodily imperfec-
tions that hemmed him in so narrowly sprang
from the same source.

Whittier's formal education was scarcely
greater than that of an ordinary country boy.
He learned to read at home, and then attended
the district school for periods proportionately
less as his labor on the farm became increas-
ingly valuable. He studied there only the old
three rudiments, and those only in the strange
old ways. Both the course of study and the
method of teaching are now frowned upon by
the theorists of our time, and apparently with
reason. But there was that in the earnestness
of both pupils and teachers which made up for
many deficiencies. We must never forget that
these little villages were at that time alive with
ambition and energy, steeped in spiritual, intellectual, and physical influences that filled re-

sponsive minds with a strange force like that of electricity. Whatever boys saturated with that force touched became their own. Teachers gave more than they knew, and multitudes grew strong on what now seem the husks of learning.

Farm life at that time afforded little change of scene. Whittier knew Newburyport and the villages round about, but Boston, though only forty miles away, was to him a distant region, almost completely without influence on his life and thought. Once only, apparently, did he visit the city before he was twenty, clad in a new home-spun suit of Quaker cut, with the adornment of " boughten buttons." Even then he returned by the next day's stage, startled to find that a charming woman whom he had met at the house of a relative was an actress, and hence directly connected with the theatre, that evil place against which his mother had so strictly warned him on his departure. Perhaps, too, he was depressed and bewildered by the bustling life of the little city. In his old age he was accustomed to tell thus the tale of his discomfiture : —

" ' I wandered up and down the streets,' he used to say. ' Somehow it was n't just what I expected, and the crowd was worse and worse after I got into Washington Street; and when I got tired of being jostled, it seemed to me as if the folks might get by if I waited a little

while. Some of them looked at me, and so I
stepped into an alleyway and waited and looked
out. Sometimes there did n't seem to be so
many passing, and I thought of starting, and
then they 'd begin again. 'T was a terrible
stream of people to me. I began to think my
new clothes and the buttons were all thrown
away. I stayed there a good while.' (This was
said with great amusement.) 'I began to be
homesick. I thought it made no difference at
all about my having those boughten buttons.' " [1]

At home he had access to few books, — the
Bible, which he perforce knew as lads of to-day
can never know it, and some twenty or thirty
odd volumes, mostly the sermons, tracts, biographies, or journals of famous Friends, which
he read again and again. Nowadays we read
too much, as we eat too much ; the memory, like
the digestion, is weakened by surfeit. Then, in
times of scarcity, the mind made the most of
what it received, extracting every particle of
nutriment from the rough fare. With John
Woolman's poignant autobiography he was apparently not then acquainted, but he knew the
" tales of faith fire-winged by martyrdom " of
" painful Sewel's ancient tome," and from this,
from the " old and quaint " journal of Chalk-

[1] Mrs. James T. Fields, *Whittier, Notes of his Life and of
his Friendships*, 26.

ley, " rare sea-saint," as well as from the biographies of those unrepentant New England
rogues, Stephen Burroughs and Henry Tufts, he
learned to distinguish the warp and woof of the
great web of life. Other books came by chance.
He knew " Pilgrim's Progress," and long remembered a picture of the " evil angel, horned,
hoofed, scaly, and fire-breathing, illustrating the
tremendous encounter of Christian in the valley
where ' Apollyon straddled over the whole breadth
of the way.'" [1] He had Lindley Murray's " English Reader " and Caleb Bingham's " American
Preceptor," — to both be honor, for from each
many a youth learned the dignity and nobility
of literature. Narratives of travel and adventure he obtained from time to time from Dr.
Weld, the good old physician of " Snow-Bound,"
or from others, sometimes walking miles for the
purpose ; and once there fell into his hands one
of the Waverley novels, which he read at night
with his sister by stealth, the candle seeming
always to expire as they reached the very crisis.
Of 'good poetry, however, there was a sad lack
in the household, according to his own testimony,
although he also says that he remembers " how,
at a very early age, the solemn organ-roll of
Gray's ' Elegy' and the lyric sweep and pathos
of Cowper's ' Lament for the Royal George '

[1] *Supernaturalism of New England*, iii.

moved and fascinated me with a sense of mystery and power felt, rather than understood." In any case, it was the first great crisis of his life when he read Burns, all his imagination bursting at once into sudden flame.

The introduction came in two different ways.

"One day we had a call from a 'pawky auld carle' of a wandering Scotchman. To him I owe my first introduction to the songs of Burns. After eating his bread and cheese and drinking his mug of cider he gave us Bonny Doon, Highland Mary, and Auld Lang Syne. He had a rich full voice, and entered heartily into the spirit of his lyrics. I have since listened to the same melodies from the lips of Dempster, than whom the Scottish bard has had no sweeter or truer interpreter; but the skilful performance of the artist lacked the novel charm of the gaberlunzie's singing in the old farmhouse kitchen." [1]

"When I was fourteen years old, my first schoolmaster, Joshua Coffin, the able, eccentric historian of Newbury, brought with him to our house a volume of Burns's poems, from which he read, greatly to my delight. I begged him to leave the book with me, and set myself at once to the task of mastering the glossary of the Scottish dialect at its close. This was about

---

[1] "Yankee Gypsies," *Prose Works*, i. 336.

the first poetry I had ever read, — with the exception of that of the Bible, of which I had been a close student, — and it had a lasting influence upon me. I began to make rhymes myself, and to imagine stories and adventures. In fact, I lived a sort of dual life, and in a world of fancy, as well as in the world of plain matter-of-fact about me." [1]

Whittier's early admiration for Burns may too have been stimulated by his acquaintance with Robert Dinsmore, of the neighboring town of Windham, N. H., a Scotch farmer and verse writer and an ardent admirer and imitator of Burns, a little volume of whose simple poems was published in Haverhill in 1828 by Whittier's friend and patron, Mr. A. W. Thayer, Whittier himself contributing some Scottish verses to the "rustic bard." The downright honesty and genuine humanity of Dinsmore's work is well brought out in a delightful essay of Whittier's, written in his maturer years, a passage from which will indicate the qualities that must have influenced him as a boy : —

"He tells us of his farm life, its joys and sorrows, its mirth and care, with no embellishment, with no concealment of repulsive and ungraceful features. Never having seen a nightingale, he makes no attempt to describe the fowl; but he

[1] Autobiographical Sketch, in Appendix, i.

has seen the night hawk, at sunset, cutting the
air above him, and he tells of it.   Side by side
with his waving cornfields and orchard blooms
we have the barnyard and pigsty.   Nothing
which was to the comfort and happiness of his
home and avocation was to him 'common or
unclean.'   Take, for instance, the following, from
a poem written at the close of autumn, after the
death of his wife : —

> "'No more may I the Spring Brook trace,
>   No more with sorrow view the place
>   Where Mary's wash-tub stood ;
>   No more may wander there alone,
>   And lean upon the mossy stone
>   Where once she piled her wood.
>   'T was there she bleached her linen cloth,
>   By yonder bass-wood tree ;
>   From that sweet stream she made her broth,
>   Her pudding and her tea.
>   That stream, whose waters running,
>   O'er mossy root and stone,
>   Made ringing and singing,
>   Her voice could match alone.'

"The last time I saw him, he was chaffering in
the market-place of my native village, swapping
potatoes and onions and pumpkins for tea, coffee,
molasses, and, if the truth be told, New England
rum.   Threescore years and ten, to his own
words,

> "'Hung o'er his back,
>   And bent him like a muckle pack,'

yet he still stood stoutly and sturdily in his thick

shoes of cowhide, like one accustomed to tread independently the soil of his own acres,— his broad, honest face seamed by care and darkened by exposure to ' all the airts that blow,' and his white hair flowing in patriarchal glory beneath his felt hat. A genial, jovial, large-hearted old man, simple as a child, and betraying, neither in look nor manner, that he was accustomed to

> " ' Feed on thoughts which voluntary move
> Harmonious numbers.'

Peace to him! A score of modern dandies and sentimentalists could ill supply the place of this one honest man. In the ancient burial-ground of Windham, by the side of his ' beloved Molly,' and in view of the old meeting-house, there is a mound of earth, where, every spring, green grasses tremble in the wind and the warm sunshine calls out the flowers. There, gathered like one of his own ripe sheaves, the farmer poet sleeps with his fathers." [1]

From at least two sources, then,— from Coffin in 1821, from the wandering minstrel earlier, and later perhaps from Dinsmore,— Whittier received the gift of Prometheus, the fire that kindled him. What Burns had done in Scotland, Whittier might possibly have done in New England; but Burns's feet rested on the shoul-

---

[1] " Robert Dinsmore," in *Prose Works*, ii. 256, 259.

ders of other singers of his race, and Whittier as
a poet had no local ancestry. Unassisted, he
would have come only tardily to a realization of
the fact that the best materials for song lay
right about him ; under other influences he would
have made wider détours from the straight path.
It was thus the greatest good fortune that his
first master was Burns rather than Wordsworth
or Coleridge or Byron, or, worst of all for him,
Keats. He had already begun, as he implies
in his mature lines on Burns, to " dream of lands
of gold and pearl, of loving knight and lady,"
when he was brought firmly back to " farmer boy
and barefoot girl," and taught to see " through
all familiar things the romance underlying."

> " New light on home-seen Nature beamed,
>   New glory over Woman ;
> And daily life and duty seemed
>   No longer poor and common. . . .
>
> " O'er rank and pomp, as he had seen,
>   I saw the Man uprising ;
> No longer common or unclean,
>   The child of God's baptizing !
>
> " With clearer eyes I saw the worth
>   Of life among the lowly ;
> The Bible at his Cotter's hearth
>   Had made my own more holy."

Children like to rhyme, the juxtaposition of
words of similar sound delighting them much as
plays on words do simple people of a later

growth; but the taste soon disappears. In Whittier it was more permanent. As a small boy he covered his slate with verses, instead of with sums, when he sat by the hearth in the evening; and apparently soon passed from the first stage, doggerel, into the second, imitation of the occasional verses he found in the poetical corner of the weekly paper or in the school reader. By 1823 he showed both talent and practice, for some lines in an album, of which the following are part, bear that date : —

" When our moments of youth are glided away,
When the pleasures of youth are sunk in decay,
When the hopes we have cherished and the joys we have known
Oblivion has covered and time overthrown,
If these lines come before thee, thy memory may cast
Through the wreck of long years a dim thought of the past,
Thou mayst think upon him who thus feebly has penned
The lines here annexed to the name of a friend."

Here he has caught the swing of long lines as neatly as in "The Willows," a poem of about the same time, he reached the full spirit of Woodworth's "Old Oaken Bucket," — which, though not itself original in form, had proved sufficiently original in matter to become at once a great favorite. Whittier's verses are palpably imitative, but not basely so. The main idea is another's; its application in detail is his own, and the adjectives do credit to his growing power of selection.

" Oh, dear to my heart are the scenes which delighted
  My fancy in moments I ne'er can recall,
When each happy hour new pleasures invited,
  And hope pictured visions more holy than all.
Then I gazed with light heart, transported and glowing,
  On the forest-crowned hill and the rivulet's tide,
O'ershadowed with tall grass and rapidly flowing
  Around the lone willow that stood by its side, —
The storm-battered willow, the ivy-bound willow, the water-
  washed willow that grew by its side."

A careful examination of these verses, of the
half dozen or more others written between 1823
and 1825, and of the dozen or more written in
1826–27, make it clear that Burns had served
more to stimulate Whittier's imagination than to
lead him into special lines of imitation.   There
are extant a dozen pieces or so in the Scotch dialect, mostly of the humorous sort; but they were
not his earliest work nor his best.   The impel-
ling power and the range of thought suggested
may have come from Burns, but not the form,
which he took from the current models most
accessible.

An imitation of Moore, "The Exile's Departure," beginning "Farewell, shores of Erin,
green land of my Fathers," which he wrote
June 1, 1825, was the occasion of a new crisis
in his life, for it brought him into relations with
William Lloyd Garrison, a boy only two years
older than himself, destined for a long period to
be respected by few and detested by many, but

clearly the most powerful influence acting in American public life between 1830 and 1850. Unknown to Whittier, his sister Mary sent this poem to Garrison's paper, the Newburyport "Free Press," where it appeared on June 8, 1826, to his own huge delight. He himself then sent another piece, in blank verse, "The Deity," based on 1 Kings xix. 11, 12, and that was printed with the following paragraph prefixed : —

"The author of the following graphic sketch, which would do credit to riper years, is a youth of only sixteen, who we think bids fair to prove another Bernard Barton, of whose persuasion he is. His poetry bears the stamp of true poetic genius, which, if carefully cultivated, will rank him among the bards of his country." [1]

Garrison was only remotely of Essex County stock. His grandfather was an Englishman who had settled in New Brunswick and had married a daughter of an emigrant from the Newburyport region. His father had married a girl of mingled English and Irish ancestry, and a roving life had brought him to Newburyport. The son thus represented a far later tide of immigration than that which bore the Whittiers to Essex County ; but he had the strength of mind that befits a pioneer, and it fell to his iron will and indomitable energy to lead a great moral

[1] Pickard, *Life*, i. 51.

revolution. Virtually self-educated and forced from childhood to earn his own support, he had while a printer's apprentice mastered the mysteries of the editor's craft and trained himself to think and write on public affairs. His apprenticeship over, his unselfish employer helped him to start a rival journal, the "Free Press," which was to be neutral in its politics. Its motto was "Our Country, Our Whole Country, and nothing but Our Country," and its frankness, honesty, and humanity commended it to the elder Whittier, old-fashioned anti-slavery Quaker Democrat that he was, and brought it at once into his household.

What followed must be told in Garrison's own words: —

"Going upstairs to my office one day, I observed a letter lying near the door, to my address; which, on opening, I found to contain an original piece of poetry for my paper, the 'Free Press.' The ink was very pale, the handwriting very small; and, having at that time a horror of newspaper 'original poetry,' — which has rather increased than diminished with the lapse of time, — my first impulse was to tear it in pieces, without reading it, the chances of rejection, after its perusal, being as ninety-nine to one; . . . but, summoning resolution to read it, I was equally surprised and gratified to find it above medi-

ocrity, and so gave it a place in my journal. . . .
As I was anxious to find out the writer, my
post-rider one day divulged the secret — stating
that he had dropped the letter in the manner
described, and that it was written by a Quaker
lad, named Whittier, who was daily at work on
the shoemaker's bench, with hammer and lap-
stone, at East Haverhill. Jumping into a vehicle, I lost no time in driving to see the youthful
rustic bard, who came into the room with shrink-
ing diffidence, almost unable to speak, and blush-
ing like a maiden. Giving him some words of
encouragement, I addressed myself more particularly to his parents, and urged them with great
earnestness to grant him every possible facility
for the development of his remarkable genius. . . .

" Almost as soon as he could write, he [Whit-
tier] gave evidence of the precocity and strength
of his poetical genius, and when unable to procure paper and ink, a piece of chalk or charcoal
was substituted. He indulged his propensity for
rhyming with so much secrecy (as his father
informed us) that it was only by removing some
rubbish in the garret, where he had concealed
his manuscripts, that the discovery was made.
This bent of his mind was discouraged by his
parents : they were in indigent circumstances,
and unable to give him a suitable education,
and they did not wish to inspire him with hopes

which might never be fulfilled. . . . We endeavored to speak cheeringly of the prospects of
their son; we dwelt upon the impolicy of war-
ring against nature, of striving to quench the
first kindlings of a flame which might burn like
a star in our literary horizon, and we spoke, too,
of fame. 'Sir,' replied his father, with an emotion which went home to our bosom like an
electric shock, 'poetry will not give him bread.'
What could we say? The fate of Chatterton,
Otway, and the whole catalogue of those who
had perished by neglect, rushed upon our memory, and we were silent." [1]

The "Free Press" was an unsuccessful venture and was discontinued in September, and
shortly afterwards Garrison left Newburyport
to seek his fortune in Boston. But his advice
to give Whittier an education was reiterated in
January, 1827, by Abijah W. Thayer, the editor
of the Haverhill "Gazette," to which Whittier
had been sending his poems. This time the
father, realizing that the injury Whittier had received prevented his becoming a robust farmer,
consented, on condition that the son should earn
the means, for the farm was mortgaged, and
ready money not to be obtained otherwise than
by the boy's own efforts. A way lay just at
hand. Shoemaking was one of the great in-

[1] *William Lloyd Garrison: the Story of his Life*, i. 67.

dustries of the county, and in the absence of machinery was then carried on more by home labor than by factory work. Whittier had learned from a hired man on the farm the art of making slippers of a certain kind, and had practised it previously, if Garrison's memory be not at fault; at any rate he now took it up with vigor. One of his teachers in the district school thus describes him at his work :—

" If my memory serves me rightly, Mr. Whittier, with others on the farm, made shoes in one of those little shops you see now at country farmhouses. I remember that he used to sit on a low bench that had a little draw [drawer] at the side. When I have entered the shop for a chat with those I was sure to find there, I remember that often Mr. Whittier would pull out the little draw and hand me some loose sheets of paper, with the poems he had written on them during the day. He usually offered no comment, but continued steadily at his work." [1]

In the winter and spring of 1827 the young artisan earned enough to pay his carefully calculated expenses at the new Haverhill Academy, at the dedication of which, on April 30, an ode of his composing was sung. For the summer term of six months he jubilantly carried

[1] Moses E. Emerson, quoted in W. S. Kennedy, *J. G. Whittier*, American Reformers Series, 49.

on his studies, living in the family of Mr. Thayer and returning to the farm every Friday night. He pursued the ordinary branches, with the addition of French, astonishing his master by his excellence in English composition. He was a favorite among his fellows of both sexes, who appreciatively passed his manuscript verses from hand to hand. He now had for the first time access to libraries, and revelled in their contents, for his mind had been hitherto but frugally, not to say scantily, fed; and as the young poet of the village he was welcomed and made much of everywhere. In the winter of 1827–28 he replenished his exhausted resources in a more traditional way by teaching school in the Birch Meadow district, now Merrimac, which lies between his home and Amesbury, and in the spring of 1828 returned to the academy for another and final term. At its conclusion he had of course only the rudiments of a sound education, not to be compared with the comparatively elaborate equipment of Longfellow, Holmes, Lowell, Emerson, and Thoreau. But he had found the way to a knowledge of literature and history, and he knew as much as many of the editors and not a few politicians of his time.

Meanwhile he had been writing verse and prose with great activity. In 1827 and 1828 about a hundred of his poems were printed in the "Gazette," besides articles on temperance, on Robert Burns, and on war, and one, in the Boston "Philanthropist," on gambling. He was still in the imitative stage, learning his art through a series of enthusiasms that corresponded to his wider opportunities for reading. When he entered the academy, he was evidently a devotee of Moore, or at least of that swelling and rhetorical verse which we associate with Moore's name, as is shown by the ode sung at the dedication, beginning "Hail, Star of Science, come forth in thy splendor." But from about that time his style and choice of subjects shifted rapidly. Sometimes he imitated Willis, who was then attracting attention by scriptural sketches, sometimes Bryant, as when he writes:

> " Drear place of dreamless solitude ! to thee
>   Earth's generations pass. The small, the great,
>   The mighty monarch and his meanest slave,
>   Unceremonious mix their equal dust
>   Within thy gloom-wrapt mansions."

But his chief exemplar was certainly Mrs. Hemans. In fact, she seems to have been the favorite poet of the district. Garrison quoted her verses in the "Free Press" more frequently than those of any one else; Thayer in the "Gazette" had the same habit until Whittier became his versifier in ordinary; and Whittier's sister, in a scrap-book of this period, mingles

Mrs. Hemans's verses with those written by her brother. Whittier followed Mrs. Hemans closely in style and subjects, as may be seen by the opening lines of " Pericles at the Bier of his Son " : —

> " Stand back ! stand back ! ye mourners all !
>   The father of the dead
>   Comes up the long resounding hall
>   With slow and solemn tread."

What attracted people in general in such work it is almost impossible to understand until we put ourselves in the place of a generation wholly unused to finding emotion expressed in poetry. Satiated with didactic and prosaic verse of all kinds, and just beginning to feel the thrill of romance in history, they turned with delight to anybody's versified account of anything unusual, without demanding that the moral drawn or the emotion awakened should be justified by a calm and rational judgment of the material treated. In those days the mere hint of the historian was enough to set the poet off at a gallop. Because he felt his heart stir at a romantic or pathetic situation, he must needs try to set forth the picture, the circumstances, and the characters, — all, we see now, hopelessly out of keeping with the facts in the case as revealed by more analytic and less impulsive consideration. Such was the taste of the day, of which

Mrs. Hemans was the best example, and to her Whittier owed the stimulus for poems on " Pericles at the Bier of his Son," " Eve at the Burial of Abel," " Montezuma's Defiance of Cortes," " Sardanapalus's Reproof of his Courtiers," " The Death of Ossian," and many another.

It is small wonder that Whittier's verse was at once received with approbation by his neighbors and townsmen. They simply recognized that a poet had arisen among them who met their tastes, who touched their emotions. They had little with which to compare his verse, and they properly gave it their highest praise. In the " Gazette," January 13, 1827, Mr. Thayer said: —

" The author of the following effusions, to whom we have before been indebted for contributions to the poetical department of our paper, we understand is a young man only seventeen [twenty] years of age, an apprentice to the shoemaking business, and possessing no other advantages of education than are afforded in the common town schools. If nature or the ' sacred nine ' inspire him to write such poetry under his present disadvantages we surely have reason to expect much from him, should his genius be assisted by a classical education."

On March 17 he returns to the subject: —

" His effusions . . . indicate, we should say, considering his disadvantages, a genius unparalleled among American poets. Such richness and sublimity of language and brilliancy of imagery and delicacy of sentiment have not, we believe, distinguished any of the early productions of the most celebrated modern poets."

There was local blame as well as praise. In the comment last mentioned Mr. Thayer called attention to the fact that there had been "illiberal criticism." Whittier was said "to borrow largely from other poets,"— as indeed, from a broad point of view, it was clear that he had done. Mr. Thayer defended him by declaring that "this remark (totally destitute of foundation) doubtless originated with some of those would-be critics who plume themselves on their superior education, derived, probably, from 'a six-months' sojourn at an academy.'"

But if such criticism left its sting, Whittier must have felt proud of the uniform approval which his verses met elsewhere. Many of them appeared in the Boston "Statesman" and were copied — surest sign of favor — into other journals, far and near, until the schoolboy poet came to have, even then, the beginnings of a national reputation, such as Bryant and Percival had already achieved and Willis was rapidly gaining. Under these circumstances it seemed wise to try the venture of publishing by subscription a little volume of his verse, which might add to his growing fame and contribute to his empty purse. In January, 1828, therefore, Mr. Thayer announced in the " Gazette " the proposed publication of " The Poems of Adrian," a pseudonym often used by Whittier. The following was the prospectus : —

" THE POEMS OF ADRIAN. — Many of the poems now proposed to be published originally appeared in the ' Essex Gazette,' and were very favorably received by its readers. Some of them have been copied into the most respectable papers, in various sections of the Union, with strong expressions of approbation. When the circumstances under which these poems were written are known, they will be particularly interesting. The author (a native of this town) is a young man, about nineteen years of age, who has had, until very recently, no other means of education than are afforded in a common district school, and such as he improved in the *leisure hours* of an apprenticeship to a mechanical business. It is believed by his friends that these poems indicate genius of a high order, which deserves all possible culture. The design of thus offering his juvenile writings to the public is to raise money to assist him in obtaining a classical education. He is a worthy member of the Society of Friends, and it is hoped that from them the volume will receive a liberal patronage."

The volume was to be well printed, to be bound in boards, and to contain about two hundred pages. It was to be sold for seventy-five cents, and any one securing six subscriptions was to receive a seventh copy gratis. Twenty-two subscribers had already been secured in Philadelphia. But the scheme came to naught, and with it apparently all the author's hopes of gaining money by his verse.

Lyric poetry must have a large element of autobiography, and in Whittier's schoolboy verse we find, here and there, traces of his more personal moods. He feels the injustice of men, his first experience of the world, but —

> "Though the critic's scornful eye
> Condemn his faltering lay,
> And though with heartless apathy
> The cold world turn away,
> And envy strive with secret aim
> To blast and dim his rising fame,"

still he vowed faithfulness to his humble muse. The pangs and joys of youthful love, too, were not absent. Like his Scottish prototype, or like any manly young New England farmer, he was highly susceptible to the charms of women, and like every country lad before or since, he was soon successively in love with more than one of his schoolmates. Such attachments are innocent and natural and rarely lead to marriage, but with ecstasies come jealousies, and plighted vows are followed by remorse. Whittier was a poor boy and marriage was out of the question; he was a good Quaker, too, and marriage outside of his sect was not to be thought of. But these early loves, — and one in particular, — we may find echoing faintly through his later verse; in his verse of this period they are plainly evident, particularly when, as seems to be the case, Byron gave him the clue to a pessimistic poetry in which remorse and despair go hand in hand, and he sang of blighted affection:

> " Wherefore ask me to forget
> How we loved and how we met ? . . .
> Fare thee well since others now
> Clothe in smiles thy winning brow.
> Smile on them, but thou shalt know
> Yet the deeper stings of woe."

We must not leave his schoolboy verses, however, without referring to the one poem of real excellence that belongs to that period, " The Song of the Vermonters," now included in the Appendix to his poetical works. It was intended, he said sixty years later, as " a piece of boyish mystification," and was published anonymously. Copied far and wide, it was often credited to Ethan Allen. No one with ears to hear could have believed it to have been an eighteenth century production, but no one with the faintest appreciation of verse could have read without a stirring of the blood such lines as

"Ho — all to the borders ! Vermonters, come down,
  With your breeches of deerskin and jackets of brown;
  With your red woolen caps, and your moccasins, come,
  To the gathering summons of trumpet and drum,"

or the spirited stanzas that follow. Here there was not a trace of Mrs. Hemans and her scrap-book method. In form it was purely Byronic; but the young author, grown wise for an unconscious instant, had seized hold of the one kind of material that he could really handle, — the spirit and glory of New England and her love of freedom. It was, though he did not realize it, the first sign of his greatness.

But schooldays had come to an end. Either he must prepare for college (and he had little or no Latin), and gird himself for a long struggle with poverty while carrying on his general or professional training; or look forward to an eternity of village school-teaching; or go back to the farm and slipper-making; or try his fortune as an editor. A chance in this last direction seemed to present itself, late in 1828, when his first patron, Garrison, who had gone from Newburyport to Boston, and was editing the "Philanthropist," suggested to the publisher, the Rev. William Collier, that Whittier should succeed him. The following passages from a letter to Mr. Thayer, to whom he naturally turned for advice, show his dilemma and his ambition : —

SHAD PARISH, 28th of 11th mo., 1828.

FRIEND A. W. THAYER, — I have been in a quandary ever since I left thee, whether I had better accept the offer of Friend Collier, or *nail* myself down to my seat, — for, verily, I could not be kept there otherwise, — and toil for the honorable and truly gratifying distinction of being considered "a good cobbler." . . . No — no — friend, it won't do. Thee might as well catch a weasel asleep, or the Old Enemy of Mankind in a parsonage-house, as find me contented with that distinction.

I have renounced college for the good reason that I have no disposition to humble myself to meanness for an education — crowding myself through college upon the charities of others, and leaving it with a debt or an obligation to weigh down my spirit like an incubus, and paralyze every exertion. The professions are already crowded full to overflowing — and I, forsooth, because I have a miserable knack of rhyming, must swell the already enormous number, struggle awhile with debt and difficulties, and then, weary of life, go down to my original insignificance, where the tinsel of classical honors will but aggravate my misfortune. Verily, friend Thayer, the picture is a dark one — but from my heart I believe it to be true. What, then, remains for me? School-keeping — out upon it! The memory of last year's experience comes up before me like a horrible dream. No, I had rather be a tin-peddler, and drive around the country with a bunch of sheepskins hanging to my wagon. I had rather hawk essences from dwelling to dwelling, or practise physic between Colly Hill and Country Bridge [the most sparsely settled portion of the East Parish].

Seriously — the situation of editor of the "Philanthropist" is not only respectable, but it is peculiarly pleasant to one who takes so deep an interest, as I really do, in the great cause it is laboring to promote. I would enter upon my task with a heart free from misanthropy, and glowing with that feeling that wishes well to all. I would rather have the memory of a Howard, a Wilberforce, and a Clarkson than the undying fame of Byron.[1]

[1] Pickard, *Life*, i. 70.

CHAPTER III

THUS through the early distinction of his verse had Whittier been drawn from the peaceful and remote life of the farm and the Quaker household into the more worldly life of a busy little town. His ambition aroused, and a taste for the pleasures and profits of the world awakened, it must have seemed as if return to the former state would be almost like annihilation. It was apparently with delight, therefore, that he embraced the unexpected opportunity to edit a Boston paper, and thus began a second brief cycle in his career, — three years in which he tried to speak the language and live the life of this strange outer world, to cherish its ambitions and enjoy as best he could its pleasures, only in the end, as we shall see, to be brought inevitably back to the quiet rural district which had moulded him and had already signed and sealed him as its own.

An editorship was not then a post of great distinction. Garrison, the editor of the " Philan-

thropist," roomed with its printer at a boarding-
house kept by the owner, Collier, a Baptist
" city missionary ; " and the paper, noble as were
its aims and able as was Garrison's handling of
it, was a mere experiment.   As it turned out, it
was not even the " Philanthropist " that Whittier
was to take charge of, but another weekly journal just established by the Colliers, the " American Manufacturer," " devoted to the interests of
manufactures, mechanics, agriculture, internal
improvements, literature, education, and general
intelligence."   With volume one, number 14,
January 1, 1829, this paper began to bear his
name at the head of its editorial columns, Mr.
Collier announcing in the same issue that he had
relinquished the editorship and that the journal
would be in future "conducted by John G.
Whittier, who is well known to the public as a
writer of promise."

Whittier's salary was only nine dollars a
week, and it seems to have been understood that
he should board with his employer.   A large
part of the " Manufacturer " was taken up with
routine matter, — " current prices wholesale" and
the like, — and Whittier's main duty was apparently the concoction of a few editorials, which
were for a while of a sufficiently general character
to serve equally well for the " Philanthropist,"
then without an editor.   He salutes the new year :

"Another year has been chronicled with the
dead. One portion of our earthly existence has
gone by, and another, big with unknown events,
is opening before us." He contemplates the
thought of death, he advocates the cause of temperance, he rebukes infidelity. With better
success he treats of the authors of the day. In
the issue of January 8 he has an article on the
novels of Sir Walter Scott. "Several of these
volumes," he says, "which have been produced
with such wonderful rapidity and unexampled
success, have in our opinion a tendency to sub-
vert some of the purest principles of Christian
Morality. . . . Our sympathies are enlisted frequently on the wrong side, yet we cannot avoid
it, for a fascination is around us, — the fascination of glowing narrative and masterly delinea-
tion of character. The wassail-feast, the Bac-
chanalian revel, the drunken exploits of profane
and licentious cavaliers, are described in a manner ill-calculated to produce a salutary impression upon the mind."

On the other hand, he is greatly moved by
Croly's "Salathiel," which has been recently
revived under the title, "Tarry Thou till I
Come;" he quotes liberally from Dana's "Buc-
caneer;" and he speaks with entire approval of
L. E. L., then the darling of the general reading public in England: "She has laid open to

the world the secrets of a heart exquisitely alive
to earnest and clinging affections, with too much
minuteness, with too much truth. She has described love as a wild and all-engrossing passion,
instead of repressing it."

The "Manufacturer" had been established to
further the interests of the new protective tariff
and of Clay's "American system," so advan-
tageous to New England and so perplexing to
the South. Whittier was ignorant of political
economy, and indeed he must needs have been
very wise to have found his way through the
tangle of tariff discussion at that time. But
luckily the policy of the paper was consonant
with ideas which had long been familiar to him
in the manufacturing district of the Merrimac
valley, and it was natural for a Quaker to be
dissatisfied with the warlike Jackson and to deny
his fitness for the presidency. As the weeks
went by, he grew more at ease in his new func-
tion, and on April 16 he felt himself sufficiently
master of the situation to begin a series of editorial addresses " to the young mechanics of New
England : " " The person who now addresses you
has been ranked among your number. Called
to another sphere of action, he retains a sincere
regard for the welfare of his former associates —
those companions of his early years, whom he
is proud to recognize as his friends. From indi-

viduals, his regard is now extended to all who are included in that class of the community to whom this article is addressed. He has felt, in common with you all, the injustice of that illiberal feeling, which has been manifested towards mechanics by the wealthy and arrogant of other classes. He has felt his cheek burn, and his pulse quicken, when witnessing the open, undisguised contempt with which his friends have been received — not from any defect in their moral character, their minds, or their persons, but simply because they depended upon their own exertions for their means of existence, and upon their own industry and talents for a passport to public favor." In five addresses of this sort the young editor counselled work, thought, and self-control to his brethren in the mechanic arts, and pleaded with them to renew the old preeminence of New England by their industry and their virtue.

If his contract called only for prose, he certainly exceeded its limits, for he contributed to the " Manufacturer " not only many non-political poems but a series of poetical skits called " Tariffiana," and he sent to the Cincinnati " American " some good verses on Clay, — in answer to the current charge that Clay and Jackson had united in a political " deal," — which were widely circulated during the ensuing presidential campaign.

His editorial duties, however, were no great
tax on his mind or his time, and he had leisure
for reading and his friends. He was in reality,
as he said many years later, a shy and timid recluse, afraid of a shadow, especially the shadow
of a woman; but he was bravely endeavoring to
live as others did in a world of pretenses, as may
be gathered from letters of that period : —

"Here I have been all day trying to write
something for my paper, but what with habitual
laziness, and a lounge or two in the Athenæum
Gallery, I am altogether unfitted for composition. . . . There are a great many pretty girls at
the Athenæum, and I like to sit there and remark upon the different figures that go flitting
by me, like aërial creatures just stooping down
to our dull earth, to take a view of the beautiful
creations of the painter's genius. I love to watch
their airy motions, notice the dark brilliancy of
their fine eyes, and observe the delicate flush
stealing over their cheeks, but, trust me, my
heart is untouched, — cold and motionless as a
Jutland lake lighted up by the moonshine. I
always did love a pretty girl. Heaven grant
there is no harm in it! . . . Mr. Garrison will
deliver an address on the Fourth of July. He
goes to see his Dulcinea every other night almost, but is fearful of being 'shipped off,' after
all, by her. Lord help the poor fellow, if it

happens so. I like my business very well; but hang me if I like the people here. I am acquainted with a few girls, and have no wish to be so with many." [1]

. . . "I have become a notable fellow in gallantry of late; I mean old-fashioned gallantry, however. I have given my whiskers a more ferocious appearance, and take the liberty of frightening into good nature those who will not be complacent of their own accord." [2]

There were bickerings and jealousies in the boarding-house and the printing-house of the Colliers, and Whittier was probably somewhat relieved when in August, 1829, he was called home by the severe illness of his father. The old man lived until June, 1830, but upon Whittier devolved the management of the farm and for the present it seemed that his progress as an editor was barred. Fortunately he was soon offered the editorship of the Haverhill "Gazette," which had during his absence in Boston reprinted many of his poems; had praised his articles in the "Manufacturer,"— which reveal "all the warmth of language and richness of imagination" so peculiarly characteristic of its editor's mind; had set him as a poet and a man above Willis, who was still growing in popular favor; and had quoted

[1] Pickard, *Life*, i. 93.
[2] Pickard, *Life*, i. 78, note.

from the Philadelphia "Ladies' Literary Gazette" an "Ode to J. G. Whittier," signed Henriqueta, declaring that "*thou* art one whom aftertime shall hallow with its fame."

For the first six months of 1830 Whittier edited the "Gazette." It was a weekly sheet, containing but little original matter, and his duties did not interfere with his residence on the farm or his labors there. Once, indeed, he announced that "the Editor, being unexpectedly absent during the whole of the present week, was of course unable to attend to this number of the 'Gazette.'" His poetical contributions appeared with frequency, and his political editorials were serious and sensible, though noticeably less enthusiastic than those he wrote for the "Manufacturer." The most characteristic was that of March 20, which praised "the bold and rich eloquence" of an article in the "New England Review" on New England military heroes, and went on to laud New England as "the native home of the intellect" and as noble through her manifestations of moral power, her free institutions, and her religion.

This praise of the "New England Review," of Hartford, Conn., was synchronous with certain contributions to it, and with an epistolary friendship with its editor, George D. Prentice, a dashing young fellow, quite the opposite of Whittier,

as was apparent from his later career as editor
of the Louisville "Journal," but at that period
probably Whittier's ideal of what a successful
journalist and politician ought to be. They had
never met, but Prentice wrote thus to him, in the
braggadocio style of the time, after describing
how he stole a kiss from a young poetess : —

"Whittier, I wish you were seated by my
side, for I assure you that my situation, just
now, is very much to my particular satisfaction.
Here am I in my hotel, with a good-natured fire
in front of me, and a bottle of champagne at my
left hand. Can you imagine a situation more
to a good fellow's mind? . . . Then you have
more imagination than judgment. . . . The
gods be praised that I am not a member of the
temperance society !

"Would to fortune I could come to Haverhill
before my return to Hartford — but the thing is
impossible. I am running short both of time
and money. Well, we can live on and love, as
we have done. Once or twice I have even
thought that my feelings towards you had more
of romance in them than they possibly could
have if we were acquainted with each other. I
never yet met for the first time with a person
whose name I had learned to revere, without
feeling on the instant that the beautiful veil
with which my imagination had robed him was

partially rent away.   If you cannot explain this
matter, you are no philosopher." [1]

The "New England Review" was a Clay
paper, and Prentice's slashing articles attracted
so much attention that he was asked to go to
Kentucky for the purpose of writing a biography
of Clay, which was needed for the coming presidential campaign.   Prentice recommended that
Whittier take his place on the "Review," and
a proposal to this effect was made by the own-
ers, who offered a salary of five hundred dollars
a year.   It was accepted by Whittier, and in
July, 1830, he began his new duties at Hartford,
thus heralded by his predecessor in his valedic-
tory address : —

"I cannot do less than congratulate my readers on the prospect of their more familiar acquaintance with a gentleman of such powerful
energies and such exalted purity and sweetness
of character.   I have made some enemies among
those whose good opinion I value, but no rational
man can ever be the enemy of Mr. Whittier."

The verses and tales which Whittier contributed to the "Review" we must reserve for later
consideration.   Our business now lies with his
success in his profession.   On the "Manufacturer" he had been a novice ; on the "Gazette"
he had through experience learned confidence ;

[1] Pickard, *Life,* i. 80.

but both positions were narrow and inconspicuous compared with that which he now held. Here his editorials were excellent: they showed the crude sectionalism of the time, but they were dignified and vigorous. He praised Webster's rebuke to nullification: " Last session of Congress was a proud one for New England — for the whole country. The North was assailed with the usual bitterness — but not as usual with impunity. A giant was called up — one who had borne until forbearance was not longer his duty. He shook himself free of sectional prejudices ; and he spoke for the whole country — for posterity." He upheld the tariff: " New England has within herself resources — springs of wealth and incentive to enterprise." The party should therefore rally around Clay, " who has sustained with a giant's strength the best interests of the country." . . . The South is merely jealous of the North ; she is really benefited by the tariff of abominations on account of the increase of ten per cent in the value of agricultural products." He bewailed the corrupt administration and lauded " the upright and unbending politician — the eloquent and soul-reaching orator — the dignified statesman — the accomplished gentleman — the unwavering advocate of the people — *Henry Clay*. To him we look for our political redemption ; to him we turn in this dark day of our national existence, with a strong hope and an earnest confidence."

It must be borne clearly in mind that at this period Whittier was merely a young New England journalist, a journalist of austere breeding and with a tendency toward philanthropy, but not by any means yet a reformer. A private letter of the period shows that he was far from being ready to take up the cause of the slave, whom he sometimes regarded rather as a nuisance than as an oppressed creature ; and in his contributions to his paper, though he praised Garrison's stand in the matter of abolition, he did not himself appear to take any greater interest in this reform than in others. His attitude was well expressed in an editorial of September 20, 1830 : " I shall endeavor to aid the cause of morality and national religion. A moral revolution is going on around us — the voice of public opinion is growing louder, and already the strongholds of Vice are shaking to its responses, like the walls of Jericho to the sound of the trumpet. I shall seek to promote this glorious revolution. I trust I shall never so far prostitute the intellect which God has given me, as to become the apologist of immorality and irreligion, whatever shape they may assume, or under whatever name they may appear."

In March, 1831, Whittier was called back to

Haverhill to assist in the settlement of his father's estate, and while there fell ill. He conducted the "Review" from this distance for some time, returned for a brief period to Hartford, and then went back to the farm, resigning his editorship with the end of 1831.

His experience in Hartford had been stimulating and valuable in every way. In Boston he had been at a disadvantage. He was connected with an obscure paper and associated, to a great degree, with obscure people. His reputation as a poet, already considerable, would have enabled him eventually to make better connections,[1] but the time of his sojourn was too short. In Hartford he found himself at the head of a well-established and somewhat distinguished journal, and was at once received into a compact and brilliant society with strong literary interests. The memory of the Hartford Wits still lingered, and a new circle, composed of men and women of solid acquirements and genuine attractiveness, had gathered up around Percival, Brainard, and

[1] "At that time, 1826, Boston was notoriously the literary metropolis of the Union — the admitted Athens of America. . . . Society was strongly impressed with literary tastes; genius was respected and cherished: a man, in those days, who had achieved literary fame, was at least equal to the president of a bank, or a treasurer of a manufacturing company." — S. G. Goodrich, *Recollections of a Lifetime*, Letter 45.

Mrs. Sigourney.[1] He met the chief men of his
party, he visited New York on a confidential
political errand, and there became acquainted
with brother editors of larger fame and responsibility ; in short, he grew rapidly as a man,
under these favorable influences, and advanced
rapidly in professional reputation.

Among the young women of this charming
circle he was particularly impressed by Miss Cornelia Russ, daughter of Judge Russ, with whose
household he was on intimate terms.   When

[1] " It was, I believe, through Mr. Wadsworth's influence that
Miss Huntley, now Mrs. Sigourney, was induced to leave her
home in Norwich, and make Hartford her residence.   This
occurred about the year 1814.   Noiselessly and gracefully she
glided into our young social circle, and ere long was its presid-
ing genius.   I shall not write her history, nor dilate upon her
literary career — for who does not know them both by heart ?
Yet I may note her influence in this new relation — a part of
which fell upon myself.   Mingling in the gayeties of our social
gatherings, and in no respect clouding their festivity, she led
us all toward intellectual pursuits and amusements.   We had
even a literary cotery under her inspiration, its first meetings
being held at Mr. Wadsworth's.   I believe one of my earliest
attempts at composition was made here.   The ripples thus begun extended over the whole surface of our young society,
producing a lasting and refining effect.   It could not but be
beneficial thus to mingle in intercourse with one who has the
angelic faculty of seeing poetry in all things, and good everywhere.   Few persons living have exercised a wider influence
than Mrs. Sigourney ; no one that I now know can look back
upon a long and earnest career of such unblemished benefi-
cence." — S. G. Goodrich, *Recollections of a Lifetime*, Letter
37.

about to leave Hartford, he addressed her in the following letter,[1] in which admiration and caution are oddly mingled : —

Thursday Afternoon.

MISS RUSS, — I could not leave town without asking an interview with you. I know that my proposal is abrupt — and I cannot but fear that it will be unwelcome. But you will pardon me. About to leave Hartford for a distant part of the country, I have ventured to make a demand for which, under any other circumstances, I should be justly censurable. I feel that I have indeed no claims on your regard. But I would hope, almost against any evidence to the contrary, that you might not altogether discourage a feeling which has long been to me as a new existence. I would hope that in my absence from my own New England, whether in the sunny South or the "Far West," one heart would respond with my own — one bright eye grow brighter at the mention of a — name, which has never been, and I trust never will be, connected with dishonor, — and which, if the Ambition which now urges onward shall continue in vigorous exercise, shall yet be known widely and well — and whose influence shall be lastingly felt. —

But this is dreaming, — and it may only call

[1] Published by Professor W. L. Phelps, in the *Century Magazine*, May, 1902.

forth a smile.   If so — I have too high an opinion of your honorable feelings to suppose even
for a moment that you would make any use of
your advantage derogatory to the character of a
high-minded, and ingenuous girl ——

— I leave town on Saturday.   Can you allow
an interview this evening or on that of Friday?
If however you cannot consistently afford me the
pleasure of seeing you — I have only to resign
hopes dear to me as life itself, and carry with me
hereafter the curse of disappointed feeling.—

A note in answer will be waited for impa-
tiently.   At least you will not deny me this.

Yrs. most truly —

J. G. WHITTIER.

The reply to this epistle has not been preserved, but it was certainly a negative one. This
love of Whittier's was not his first nor was it
destined to be the last.   Handsome in person,
sensitive in nature, he craved the sympathy and
affectionate companionship that woman gives
best, and this failure to establish a connection
which esteem and admiration dictated, and which
would have made permanent his relations with
a social circle so pleasing, was another of the
disappointments that now overwhelmed him.

On his return to Haverhill Whittier may well
have felt in despair. Various plans, one of going

to the West, and another of attending as a delegate a convention of the National Republican
party at Baltimore, which was to nominate Clay
for the presidency, had to be given up on account
of illness. A rejected lover, cut off from a community from which he had been so much the
gainer, and in which he had doubtless expected
to settle permanently, he was prevented by continued ill health from following his chosen profession or from engaging in any other. No wonder
he spoke of himself as half sick, half mad. The
old farm which he had left so lightly became
then a sure refuge, and he took up, so far as he
was able, his old duties, while determining on
his future course. His letters, often couched in
the jaunty style which characterized his correspondence at that period, reveal his melancholy
and the new turn which his ambitions were to
take. On January 5, 1832, he wrote as follows
to his friend Jonathan Law of Hartford : —

" Well, I have written, — or am going to, —
being the third time in which I have actually
written to you since I left Hartford, and delayed
because I expected to be the bearer of my own
epistle. I have been at home — that is to say,
in this vicinity — all the time, — half sick, half
mad. For the last fortnight I have been kept
close. Mr. Barnard has doubtless told you that
I started for Hartford about three or four weeks

since, and was obliged to return.   Now you may
suppose that I have got the 'hypo.'   No such
thing.   It is all as real as the nose on my face,
this illness of mine, — alas, too real.   Nor am I
under the cerulean influence of the blue devils
now.   The last blue-visaged imp has departed
with my exorcism ringing in his ears — ' Con-
juro te, sceleratissime, abire ad tuum locum.'
But nonsense apart, my dear sir, what shadows
we are, and what shadows we pursue !   We start
vigorously forward with something for our object
— up, up, among the very clouds; we toil on,
we sacrifice *present* ease and *present* happiness ;
we turn from *real* blessings to picture *future*
ones — unsubstantial as the fabric of the summer
cloud or the morning mist.   We press on for a
time, the overtaxed nerves relax from their first
strong tension, until the mysterious machinery
of our existence is shattered and impeded, until
the mind realizes that, chained down to material
grossness, and clogged with a distempered and
decaying mortality, it cannot rise to heaven.
Perhaps it is well — indeed we know it is — that
this should be the end of human ambition.   But,
oh, how humiliating to the vanity of our nature !

" Now, don't imagine for one moment that I
have become morose and melancholy.   Far from
it.   I am among anxious friends.   I have a
thousand sources of enjoyment, even in the

midst of corporeal suffering. I have an excellent society here to visit and receive visits from, — my early companions and those who have grown up with me, who have known me long and well. I have spent some time in Boston, Salem, Marblehead, Andover, etc., among 'brave men and fair women;' have dabbled somewhat in local politics, and am extensively popular just now on that account. The girls here are nice specimens of what girls should be. You will find a description of one or two of them in a poem which I shall send you in a few weeks, perhaps in less time, — a poem partly written at your house, and which is being published. It lay around in fragments, staring me everywhere in the face, and at last, to get rid of it, I have given it over to the bookmakers. They will have a hard bargain of it.

"Decency forgive me! I 've filled up two pages with that most aristocratic little pronoun which represents the writer of this epistle. Misery makes a man an egotist, the world over." [1]

A month later, February 2, 1832, he writes to Mrs. Sigourney: —

"The truth is, I love poetry, with a love as warm, as fervent, as sincere, as any of the more gifted worshippers at the temple of the Muses. I consider its gift as something holy and above

[1] Pickard, *Life*, i. 97.

the fashion of the world. In the language of Francis Bacon, 'The Muses are in league with Time,' — which spares their productions in its work of universal desolation. But I *feel* and know that

> ' To other chords than mine belong
> The breathing of immortal song.'

And in consequence, I have been compelled to trust to other and less pleasant pursuits for distinction and profit. Politics is the only field now open for me, and there is something inconsistent in the character of a poet and modern politician. People of the present day seem to have ideas similar to those of that old churl of a Plato, who was for banishing all poets from his perfect republic.

" Did you ever read these lines from Halleck ?

> ' But when the grass grows green above me,
>   And those who know me now and love me
>   Are sleeping by my side,
>   Will it avail me aught that men
>   Tell to the world with lip and pen
>   That I have lived and died ? —
>   *No ;* if a garland for my brow
>   Is growing, let me have it *now,*
>   While I 'm alive to wear it ;
>   And if in whispering my name
>   There 's music in the voice of fame,
>   Like Garcia, *let me hear it !* '

Now I feel precisely so. I would have fame with me *now,* — or not at all. I would not

choose between a nettle or a rose to grow over
my grave. If I am worthy of fame, I would ask
it now, — now in the springtime of my years;
when I might share its smile with the friends
whom I love, and by whom I am loved in return.
But who would ask a niche in that temple where
the *dead* alone are crowned ; where the green and
living garland waves in ghastly contrast over the
pale cold brow and the visionless eye ; and where
the chant of praise and the voice of adulation
fall only on the deafened ear of Death ?" [1]

To Mr. Law again in September, 1832 : —

" Even if my health was restored I should not
leave this place. I have too many friends around
me, and my prospects are too good to be sacrificed for any uncertainty. I have done with
poetry and literature. I can *live* as a farmer,
and that is all I ask at present. I wish you could
make me a visit, you and Mrs. Law ; our situation is romantic enough, — out of the din and
bustle of the village, with a long range of green
hills stretching away to the river ; a brook goes
brawling at their foot, overshadowed with trees,
through which the white walls of our house are
just visible. In truth, I am as comfortable as
one can well be, always excepting ill health." [2]

And to Mrs. Sigourney in January, 1833 : —

---

[1] Pickard, *Life*, i. 101.
[2] Pickard, *Life*, i. 117.

"I hope, my dear Mrs. S., you will not attribute my neglect to answer your letter, and to acknowledge my obligations for the beautiful notice of Brainard, to anything like disregard on my part. All my friends are complaining of me for not answering their letters. Continued ill health and natural indolence, and the daily duties of a large farm, *must* be my excuse. Of poetry I have nearly taken my leave, and a pen is getting to be something of a stranger to me. I have been compelled again to plunge into the political whirlpool, for I have found that my political reputation is more influential than my poetical; so I try to make myself a man of the world — and the public are deceived, but *I* am not. They do not see that I have thrown the rough armor of rude and turbulent controversy over a keenly sensitive bosom, — a heart of softer and gentler emotions than I dare expose. Accordingly, as Governor Hamilton of South Carolina says, I have 'put on athletic habits for the occasion.'" [1]

It was to political life that his ambition had plainly been tending for more than a year. The prospects that were "too good to be sacrificed for any uncertainty" were those of being sent to Congress. The situation was this. Caleb Cushing had been trying since 1826 to secure

[1] Pickard, *Life*, i. 113.

election to Congress as the representative of the North Essex District; but though the Whigs were usually in the majority, his enemies in his own party defeated his purposes until 1834. As success then depended upon majority and not mere plurality, there were seventeen congressional elections in the district between 1831 and 1833, all without avail. Mr. Cushing was willing to transfer the candidacy for the present to some person well disposed to him who could unite the party factions. Whittier's friend Edwin Harriman was then editing the Haverhill "Iris," to which Whittier often contributed articles and poems, and he was interested in a project by which Whittier should slip into Congress in Cushing's place. The following letter to him, written probably in August, 1832, will show Whittier's desire for political success and the lengths to which he was willing to go to secure it. It was plain that he wished his friends to understand that they would be the gainers by helping him, and that the success of his plan for preventing an election in November depended to some degree upon his relations with his old patron Mr. Thayer, the editor of the "Gazette," who was an anti-Cushing man, and upon the possibility of throwing dust in the eyes of both factions.

" Since conversing with you yesterday, a new

objection to our project has occurred to me:
the Constitution requires that the representative shall be twenty-five years of age. I shall
not be twenty-five till the 17th of December. So
that I would not be eligible at the *next* trial in
November. This, you will see, gives a different
aspect to the whole affair. *Perhaps*, however,
if the contest is *prolonged* till after the next
time, the project might be put in execution.

" Suppose you advocate a holding on to Mr.
C. in your Newburyport letter? Suppose, too,
that you nominate in your paper Mr. Cushing
without any one-sided convention? After the
trial in November, you can *then* use the arguments in favor of our plan which you propose to
do now; and if it suits Mr. C. he can then *request* his friends to give their votes for some
other individual for the sake of promoting peace
in the district. The Kittredge committee would
in that case probably nominate a candidate, — if
one could be found, — but, I understand Mr.
Thayer, not with the expectation of his being
elected.

" If I were nominated after the November
trial, Mr. Thayer, situated as he and I relatively
are, would support the nomination, and let the
other candidate go, as he did John Merrill.
Purdy, the ' Telegraph,' and the ' Essex Register ' would do the same.

"The truth of the matter is, the thing would be peculiarly beneficial to me, — if not at home it would be so abroad. It would give me an opportunity of seeing and knowing our public characters, and in case of Mr. Clay's election might enable me to do something for myself or my friends. It would be worth more to me *now*, young as I am, than almost any office after I had reached the meridian of life.

"In this matter, if I know my own heart, I am not entirely selfish. I never yet *deserted a friend*, and I never will. If my friends enable me to acquire influence, it shall be exerted for *their benefit*. And give me once an opportunity of exercising it, my first object shall be to evince my gratitude by exertions in behalf of those who had conferred such a favor upon me.

"If you write to Newburyport to-day, you can say that we are willing and ready to do all we can at the next trial; say, too, that the Kittredge folks will scarcely find a candidate, and that there may be a chance for Cushing better than he has yet had; that at all events it can do no harm; and that if after that trial Mr. C. sees fit to request his friends not to vote for him for the 22d Congress, there will be as good a chance then of electing a Cushing man as there is now. Say, too, if you please, that I am ready to go on with the contest, and you had better recommend mildness in the process of electioneering." [1]

The scheme fell through, but the fact remained that the men of the neighborhood had faith in him and were willing to follow his leadership. His experience in another state, his power and reputation as a writer, his alert intelligence and shrewdness in affairs, his strong principles, not only made him a power in his district but pointed to his advancement. It was at this juncture that, in 1833, when fortune seemed again smiling on his efforts, his conscience led him to ally himself definitely with the then unpopular abolitionists and thus to open for himself a career as a reformer rather than as a politician.

We must now turn aside from Whittier's work as a professional journalist to see what progress he was making in the art which was most to distinguish him thereafter. Throughout these years of changing ideals and renewed disappointment he had been contributing verse or narrative prose, almost every week, to the papers that he was editing, as well as sending much to other periodicals. The verse was greatly in excess of the prose, but the latter was by no means inconsiderable. It must be remembered that at

[1] Pickard, *Life*, i. 168.

this time Whittier's instinct led him to prose as well as to verse; he was not yet able to determine which was his distinctive medium, nor was he yet sure of the special forms, whether of prose or verse, of which he could best prove himself the master, or of the material which he could best use. In this period of experiment all that he knew was that he must write what his heart bade him. Just as Garrison, out of his passion for reform, allied himself with many an untimely movement, somewhat to the immediate detriment of the cause he had most at heart, so Whittier, in his passion for literary expression, was naturally drawn into several kinds of writing which proved to be wholly out of accord with his genius.

The least successful sort of prose which Whittier undertook to compose in these years was the half-humorous, reflective sketch, long in popular favor, from Addison and Steele down, in which the eccentric philosopher puts forth his whims and fancies. To this class belongs Whittier's " The Nervous Man," published in the " New England Magazine," in 1832 and 1833, in which with much affected learning and with a jauntiness of style wholly consonant with some of his letters of that period, he quotes Rubius Celer and Reginald Scot, and discourses on Byron, coquettes of both sexes, and a multitude of trivialities. To successful composition of this

sort real wisdom and experience in the world of
men and of ideas are necessary, and in such
qualities, Whittier, bred in seclusion and mea-
grely educated, was but a babe.

Equally unsuccessful was Whittier's attempt,
characteristic of the time, to embody moral
lessons in narrative.   We have already referred
to " The Gamester," published in 1827, in the
" Philanthropist," in which he set forth the sin
of gambling.   In " Henry St. Clair," printed in
1830 in the " New England Review," the villain
took to drink and thereupon became a high-
wayman.   A few other crude tales, of which
the " Opium Eater " is the only one preserved
in his collected works, portray similarly sudden
crimes, usually the result of intemperance, sometimes contrasted with equally shining virtues,
and it was not until after 1840 that Whittier
relinquished altogether this species of composition, to which the greatest skill in narrative
and in character-drawing are as indispensable as
is a moral purpose.   It was perhaps a work
of this general sort that would have resulted
from his plan, happily abandoned, of writing
" a work of fiction which shall have for its
object the reconciliation of the North and the
South,— being simply an endeavor to do away
with some of the prejudices which have produced
enmity between the Southron and the Yankee.

The style which I have adopted is about half-way between the abruptness of Laurence Sterne and the smooth gracefulness of W. Irving." [1]

The same deficiency in plot and character-drawing marred his attempts at pathetic narrative of the sentimental sort, after the model set by Irving in the " Sketch Book," dealing mostly with forsaken maidens and maddened lovers; a few similar experiments in tales of wonder, plagues, and Eastern marvels, published like the others anonymously, but probably to be attributed to him, in which, following Poe's predecessors, he came to the outer borders of Poe's special domain; and even the stories in which he put most heart, quaint or weird tales based on legends native to the soil.

Whittier's first book, " Legends of New England," published in Hartford in 1831, contains seven prose sketches [2] of this last kind, most of which had been published in the " New England Magazine." They all deal with local material, the white man's feud with the Indian and his strife with the beasts of the woods, the Indian's cruel rites, the fabled marvels of the wilderness.

[1] Letter to Mrs. Sigourney, February 2, 1832, in Pickard, *Life*, i. 101.

[2] " The Midnight Attack," " The Rattlesnake Hunter," "The Haunted House," " The Powwow," " The Human Sacrifice," " A Night among the Wolves," and " The Mother's Revenge." None of these was reprinted by Whittier in his *Prose Works.*

Crude in execution, they are yet good in substance, and represent as good work as was done in such unusual and homely material until, a few years later, Hawthorne began in the same magazine a series of tales similar in essence, but in which the humble facts were touched with glamour. Whittier's preface indicated that he was conscious of being a pioneer in fertile territory :

"In the following pages I have attempted to present in an interesting form some of the popular traditions and legends of New England. The field is a new one — and I have but partially explored it. New England is rich in traditionary lore — a thousand associations of superstition and manly daring and romantic adventure are connected with her green hills and her pleasant rivers. I leave the task of rescuing these associations from oblivion to some more fortunate individual, and if this little volume shall have the effect to induce such an effort, I shall at least be satisfied, whatever may be the judgment of the public upon my own humble production . . . written during the anxieties and perplexing cares attendant upon the management of a political and literary periodical."

His style, though it lacked the charm of Hawthorne's, showed the skill of the practised writer and a feeling for the picturesque : —

"And those who battled with our fathers, or

smoked the pipe of peace in their dwellings,
where are they? Where is the mighty people
which, but a little time ago, held dominion
over this fair land, from the great lakes to the
ocean? Go to the hunting grounds of Mian-
tonimah and Annawon — to the royal homes of
Massasoit and Metacom and Sassacus, and ask
for the traces and memorials of the iron race of
warriors who wrestled with the pale Yengeese
even unto death. There will perhaps remain
the ruin of their ancient forts — the fragments
of their ragged pottery — the stone-heads of
their scattered arrows; and, here and there, on
their old battle-fields, the white bones of their
slain! And these will be all — all that remain
to tell of the perished race of hunters and warriors. The red man has departed forever.
The last gleam of his Council-fire has gone up
from amidst the great oaks of the forest, and
the last ripple of his canoe vanished from the
pleasant waters bosomed among them. His
children are hastening toward the setting of the
Sun, and the ploughshare of the stranger is busy
among the bones of his fathers."

In critical and expository essays, as might
have been expected, Whittier proved himself a
much more effective workman. In 1830 he
announced in the " Gazette " his intention of
publishing " a history of Haverhill, from its first

settlement in 1640, to the present time. Our present situation affords us an ample opportunity for a thorough examination of the town records, and for obtaining such information connected with the early history of the town as may be necessary for the accomplishment of our design." On leaving Haverhill he placed such material as he had collected in the hands of B. L. Mirick, a clerk of literary tastes and aspirations, who published a "History of Haverhill" in 1832. It was a thin little volume, well written, but containing little besides extracts from the town records, or paraphrases of them, with slight comment ; and it did not refer to any part that Whittier had in its preparation. It seems probable, however, from a careful examination of the style and contents, that Whittier had a considerable share both in the selection of material and in its presentation.[1]

In the journals Whittier had edited he had occasionally remarked on the merits of current writers, native and foreign ; but the first long piece of literary criticism — indeed, his first considerable prose article that was not a fictitious narrative — was an introduction to a posthumous collection of the poems of J. G. C.

[1] The copy in Whittier's library was sent to him by Mr. Garrison, and Mr. Pickard thinks that the fact that the title-page is torn from it, reveals Whittier's indignation at the injustice done him.

Brainard, published in 1832. In this essay of thirty pages Whittier compels even the reader of to-day to recognize the charm of Brainard's character and work — his sensitive nature,[1] his

[1] When we remember Whittier's disappointment in love, known only to himself and to the subject of his addresses, we can detect a reference to his own feelings which was perhaps meant for her eye : —

"On leaving College, he returned to New London, and entered the office of his brother, William F. Brainard, Esq., as a Student at Law. While in this situation, he experienced a disappointment of that peculiar nature, which so often leaves an indelible impression upon the human heart. It probably had some influence upon the tenor of his after life. It threw a cloud between him and the sunshine ; — it turned back upon its fountain a frozen current of rebuked affections. This circumstance has been mentioned only as affording, in some measure, a solution of what might have been otherwise inexplicable in the depression of his maturer years. Perhaps there are few men of sensitive feelings and high capacities with whom something of the kind does not exist, — something which the heart reverts to with mingled tenderness and sorrow, — one master chord of feeling the tones of whose vibrations are loudest and longest, — one strong hue in the picture of existence, which blends with, and perchance overpowers all others, — one passionate remembrance, which, at times, like the rod of the Levite, swallows up all other emotions. This great passion of the heart, when connected with disappointed feeling, is not easily forgotten. Mirth, wine, the excitement of convivial intercourse, — the gayeties of fashion, — the struggles of ambition, may produce a temporary release from its presence. But a word carelessly uttered — a flower — a tone of music — a strain of poetry, —

' Striking the electric chain wherewith we are darkly bound,'

may recall it again before the eye of the mind, — and the

vein of quaint humor, his dignified bearing in
the face of approaching death, his fondness for
scenery, his love of local romance.   This last he
described in words that reveal the passion for
New England and its early history which was
yearly growing stronger within him : —

"It has been often said that the New World
is deficient in the elements of poetry and romance ; that its bards must of necessity linger
over the classic ruins of other lands ; and draw
their sketches of character from foreign sources,
and paint Nature under the soft beauty of an
Eastern sky.   On the contrary, New England is
full of Romance ; and her writers would do well
to follow the example of Brainard.   The great
forest which our fathers penetrated — the red
men — their struggle and their disappearance —
the Powwow and the War-dance — the savage
inroad and the English sally — the tale of superstition, and the scenes of Witchcraft, — all these
are rich materials of poetry.   We have indeed
no classic vale of Tempe — no haunted Parnassus — no temple, gray with years, and hallowed
by the gorgeous pageantry of idol worship — no
towers and castles over whose moonlit ruins
gathers the green pall of the ivy.   But we have

memory of the past — the glow and ardor of passion — the
hope — the fear — the disappointment — will crowd in upon
the heart."

mountains pillaring a sky as blue as that which
bends over classic Olympus : streams as bright
and beautiful as those of Greece or Italy, —
and forests richer and nobler than those which
of old were haunted by Sylph and Dryad."

The whole article shows how rapidly Whittier
was maturing. His allusions to current literature, to Wordsworth, Coleridge, Byron, Southey,
Shelley, and Sterne indicate that the boy of a
few books had in four years become well acquainted with the modern poetry of his own
tongue. And though he speaks loosely of Brainard's merit, as when he declares that he published, " week after week, poems which would
have done honor to Burns and Wordsworth," or
that a passage in the pleasant " Address to the
Connecticut River " contains " nothing dim, or
shadowy, or meagre in its outlines, — it is the
penciling of a Leonardo da Vinci, full of life
and vigor and beauty," still he has his eye fixed on
the main truth, that here was a sincere and plain
poet, who like Burns and Wordsworth wrote simply of simple things, and like a great artist aimed
to reveal a charming landscape in all its essential beauty. Another article on " New England
Superstitions " (1833) is equally well written,
and full of that special folk-lore which none
knew better than he. Here, even more plainly
than in the essay on Brainard, the affectation

and imitation of style disappears, and weakness of structure is exchanged for strength of conception and vigor of execution.   The man — the clear-thinking, simple-hearted countryman — declares himself, and we see the qualities of mind and heart that were to do good service in the cause of freedom.

Even more interesting was the progress Whittier was making in poetry, — a progress of which the ordinary reader can have no conception.   In the body of the volume of his collected poetical works appear only five poems belonging to this period, and in the Appendix only fifteen more, in all not a tithe of the verses he wrote and published.   His own attitude with regard to his early works was unduly severe, perhaps prejudiced by the quietism of his later years.   The ordinary reader is therefore unaware of the existence of a large number of verses that have almost equal claims on his attention with what is already published, and is further bewildered by the unchronological arrangement of the poems in the current edition, which presumes arbitrarily to put asunder what custom, history, and the orderly development of genius agree in uniting.

We shall fail, too, in getting a right understanding of Whittier's progress if we do not connect it with the strong feeling then generally current in America, and particularly in New

England, that America must produce a literature
of her own. Never did man more eagerly await
the birth of an heir who should complete his
happiness and perpetuate his line, than did New
England, already two centuries old, and proud
of her individuality, long for a poet who should
signally embody her in verse. Until such a genius should arise, national and community life
was barren of its crowning joy. Many were the
speculations as to the signs of his coming. The
fickle looked now here and now there; the ignorant and vain declared that not one poet but
many had already appeared. The learned and
fastidious deliberated whether there was aught
in the nature of a republic that made it sterile
in letters. Writing about 1800, Fisher Ames
said that the point at issue was whether we can
have a literature. " Our honors have not faded
— they have not even been won. Genius no
doubt exists in our country, but it exists, like
the unbodied soul on the stream of Lethe, unconscious of its powers, till the causes to excite
and the occasions to display it, shall happen to
occur. As the years roll by, with the accumu-
lation of wealth there will be an increase of the
numbers who may choose a literary leisure.
Literary curiosity will become one of the new
appetites of the nation, and as luxury advances,
no appetite will be denied. After some ages we

shall have many poor and a few rich, many
grossly ignorant, a considerable number learned,
and a few eminently learned. Nature, never
prodigal of her gifts, will produce men of genius
who will be admired and imitated."

Predictions come rapidly to pass. The age of
literary curiosity was begun in New England.
Not only in the larger centres, but in many a
village and town, students, merchants, farmers,
and factory workers alike shared in that interest
in poetry, and the cry was louder than ever for
children of the blood who should sing the deeds
of the race and voice its deeper feelings. Why
should this blessing be denied us? Are we unworthy? Is nature in this our land not noble?
Nay, said Knapp in 1829, the time has come: —

"Here nature presents her beauties in as delicate forms, and her wonders in as bold relief, as
she has in the birthplace of the muses. She has
laid the foundation of her mountains as broad,
and raised their tops as high as in the old world.
What are the Tibers and Scamanders, measured
by the Missouri and the Amazon? Or what the
loveliness of Illyssus or Avon, by the Connecticut or the Potomac? The waters of these American rivers are as pure and sweet, and their
names would be as poetical, were they as familiar to us in song, as the others, which have been
immortalized for ages. Whenever a nation wills

it, prodigies are born. Admiration and patronage create myriads who struggle for the mastery, and for the Olympick crown. Encourage the game, and the victors will come. In the smiles of publick favour, poets will arise, yea, have already arisen, whose rays of mental fire will burn out the foul stain upon our reputation, given at first by irritated and neglected genius, and continued by envy and malice — that this is the land

'Where fancy sickens, and where genius dies.'

". . . I have no hesitation in saying, that we abound in good poets, whose writings will remain to make up the literature of a future age; nor would I yield my admiration for their productions to others who are prodigal of praise whenever their works appear; but at this time I am not prepared to say whether Pierpont or Bryant be the greater poet, or whether Percival has higher claims to immortality than his brethren of the 'enchanted grounds and holy dreams;' nor whether she [Mrs. Sigourney] of 'the banks of the Connecticut,' whose strains of poetick thought are as pure and lovely as the adjacent wave touched by the sanctity of a Sabbath's morn, be equal to her tuneful sisters, Hemans and Landon, on the other side of the water, or superior to her more sprightly rivals on this." [1]

[1] Samuel L. Knapp, *Lectures on American Literature*, 187.

Whenever a nation wills it, prodigies are born. When a nation is strong and its life rich, it must create poets. The desire spread, and determination grew. In 1839 a young commencement orator at Cambridge expressed the prevalent feeling when he said : —

" We are looking abroad and back after a literature. Let us come and live, and know in living a high philosophy and faith ; so shall we find now, here, the elements, and in our own good souls the fire. Of every storied bay and cliff we will make something infinitely nobler than Salamis or Marathon. This pale Massachusetts sky, this sandy soil and raw wind, all shall nurture us. . . . Unlike all the world before us, our own age and land shall be classic to ourselves." [1]

Whittier must be regarded, then, as one of a group of New England men and women who, at the beginning of the second quarter of the century, were eagerly laboring to follow the dictates of their natures, to fulfill their ambitions, and to meet the expectation of many about them, by expressing — in ways which they could but dimly feel — the poetic sentiment of their communities. It was the birth period of the New England poets, destined to wax so strong between 1840 and 1865. They all began, as poets must, by imitation. They followed chiefly the British

[1] Quoted in T. W. Higginson, *Cheerful Yesterdays*, 166.

writers of the new, the romantic school, with
whose temper of mind and attitude toward nature and man they had much in common. It
was over the civilized world a time of emotionalism in verse. Emotionalism revealed itself in
the love of the mediæval and the oriental, —
both realms in which conventionalism seemed
absent; in the keener sentiments with which
scenery was regarded, as if the power of sight
had been stimulated and trained; in a fondness for the exquisitely beautiful, for the wild
and terrible and extraordinary; in a desire to
be thrilled by tales of madness and crime, to be
torn with sympathy for the suffering; in religious fervor and in enthusiasm for humanitarian reform. This great quickening of the emotions made Scott and Byron and Shelley and
Keats, and just as surely it declared itself in
Whittier and Longfellow and Lowell, in Hawthorne and Emerson, brother romanticists all.

Whittier's part in this movement was important. Bryant had already produced his noble
early poems, inspired by the austere life and
austere scenery surrounding him in his childhood; Lowell was a frivolous boy. Brainard,
the man of greatest promise, was dead; Willis,
although so popular, was of no real importance;
and the leaders in the obscure forward march
were Poe, Longfellow, and Whittier. To Poe,

as a disciple of Coleridge, belonged the advance on the purely artistic side, the evolution of melody. Longfellow was an avowed scholar, though destined soon to come back to poetry with the intent of creating a literature on foreign models. Whittier was the only man of genius who was attacking the problem directly.

Every step in his development is therefore of interest. We may neglect his few moralizing poems, on temperance and the like, as barren experiments, not to be renewed; and his rare attempts in the manner and matter of Coleridge — in particular a rhymed tale called the " Fire Ship," which follows closely the " Ancient Mariner," and another, " The Demon Lover," which is, with equal obviousness, inspired by " Christabel : " —

> " The dog is baying in the clear
>   Still beauty of the autumn morn ;
>   But nevermore, with heedful ear
>   And kindling eye, that dog shall hear
>   The echoes of his master's horn."

There remain two main lines of endeavor, his experiments in the style of Byron and his experiments in the style of Mrs. Hemans.

" Peter Parley " has preserved in his admirable memoirs a record of the startling effect produced in staid New England by the poems of Byron : —

" Campbell's ' Pleasures of Hope ' and Rogers'
' Pleasures of Memory ' were favorite poems from
1800 to 1815; and during the same period
'Thaddeus of Warsaw,' the 'Scottish Chiefs,'
the ' Pastor's Fireside,' by Jane Porter; ' Sand-
ford and Merton,' by Day; ' Belinda,' ' Leonora,'
' Patronage,' by Miss Edgeworth; and ' Cœlebs
in Search of a Wife,' Hannah More, were types
of the popular taste in tales and romances.   It
was therefore a fearful plunge from this elevated
moral tone in literature, into the daring if not
blasphemous skepticisms of the new poet." [1]

Many circumstances combined to bring Whittier strongly under the influence of the new
poetry and the new conception of poetic material
and poetic method.   Bred in isolation, he had
been suddenly thrust out into the jostling world;
nourished on the writings of quietists, he now
became familiar with the heart-outpourings of
more ambitious, less saintly spirits; trained to
manual labor, where reward is commensurate
with toil, he found himself suddenly in a profession in which influential connections and mental
dexterity played an important part.   A few years
before, he had been a farmer's lad, an apprentice cobbler, a schoolboy.   Now he was at the
head of a prominent journal, in communication
with party leaders.   He had been disappointed

[1] S. G. Goodrich, *Recollections of a Lifetime*, Letter 35.

in love, jeered at for his lack of social standing;[1]
he was raw, sensitive, bewildered, but fiercely
ambitious. It was no wonder that in his grop-
ings after some guide in the darkness, he laid
hold of the most powerful influence of his time,
— the rebellious and despairing Byron.

The mood of Byron is thus predominant in
his verses of 1829–1832. Commenting on Whittier's remarks on English poetry in the review
of Brainard's work, a brother editor in Hartford
remarked that his mind was evidently of the
Byronic cast, and in his letters and in his articles
are evidences of the hold which Byron held on
his imagination. Writing to a friend, a lady, in
1831, he speaks of his hatred of reserve and
cant, of his many disappointments, of his determination to be known as something else than a
writer of rhymes, of a high goal to be won in
the strife of men. To Prentice he wrote in 1830
that he has " read Byron's own relation of himself [in Moore's biography] with sorrow, with
deep anguish," and adds : —

" I am haunted by an immedicable ambition

---

[1] Joseph Snelling, in his *Truth, a New-Year's Gift for
Scribblers* (1831), had thus satirized him : —

> " The wax still sticking to his fingers' ends,
> The upstart Wh-tt-r, for example, lends
> The world important aid to understand
> What 's said, and sung, and printed in the land."

S. G. Goodrich, *Recollections of a Lifetime*, footnote, Letter 46.

— perhaps a very foolish desire of distinction, of applause, of fame, of what the world calls immortality. . . . I cannot look upon the world with kindness — however much I desire to do so. It has neglected, it has wronged me, and its idle praise is little less repulsive to me than its loud and open rebukes. Yet there is a strange passion in our nature (which I deem but the warm aspiring of an immortal mind, seeking some angelic fellowship) that suggests eternal schemes of ambition, little likely to be fulfilled. I own myself, reluctantly, subject to these influences. Deeply as I despise the follies and abhor the crimes of society, I would not depart from this sphere of trial without leaving behind me a name to be remembered when I am dust. Then whither goes the soul ! ' "

In general, much of his verse was equally Byronic. In a poem beginning " How wearily the night goes on " (1829), he complains of not being able

> " to pour the heartless strain
> Among the grovelling things of earth.'

His hopes are dead : —

> " The world has not been kind to me,
> And I have met with cold disdain, . . .
> For I have known the cold repulse
> Which wealth can offer to the low."

Hence there arises in him demoniac hatred and

the mad desire for vengeance. In his narrative poems, also, there are Byronic themes and reminiscences ; one poem at least deals with an incident in Byron's life. In " Moll Pitcher " (1832), a long narrative poem dealing with the fortune-teller of Lynn, though the form is in imitation of Scott, the substance — the witch's revenge, the madness of the heart-broken girl — is Byronic in character.   Byronic, too, is the author's thirst for fame, expressed at the opening of the second canto, though omitted in the edition of 1840 : —

> " Land of my fathers ! — if my name,
>   Now humble and unwed to fame,
>   Hereafter burn upon the lip,
>   As one of those which may not die,
>   Linked in eternal fellowship
>   With visions pure and strong and high —
>   If the wild dreams, which quicken now
>   The throbbing pulse of heart and brow,
>   Hereafter take a real form
>   Like spectres changed to being warm ;
>   And over temples worn and gray
>   The star-like crown of glory shine, —
>   Thine be the bard's undying lay,
>   The murmur of his praise be thine ! "

And to the same source seems to be due not only the form but the theme of the " Minstrel Girl " (1829), that of the famous singer whose despair at her lover's death had driven her to religious seclusion.

This predominant influence was due to the disturbing stimulus of the new and larger world, to which he was yet imperfectly adjusted, and was completely foreign to the quietism of Whittier's early training and of his later feelings. Fortunately, it was modified by two other influences, that of Scott and that of Mrs. Hemans.

Scott showed him that the richest poetical material lay in the legends of his country's past. Romantic-minded as Whittier naturally was, and versed in the local history of New England, he was thus on the verge of the discovery that the life of the olden time could be best expressed in ballad verse. The substance of splendid poems was in his mind, but the right form was wanting. The dying Indian chieftain, the helpless captive of the pirates at Marblehead, the spectre warriors and the phantom ship,— these and other themes equally striking appear in the verses collected in " Legends of New England." But the treatment was that of Scott's narrative verse, and the effect was mediocre.

Scott's influence brought Whittier more wholesome material, but his growth on the equally important side of form seems to have been due to his own long-continued practice under the influence of his old idol, Mrs. Hemans. For a time he seemed to own allegiance to the now almost forgotten sentimentalist, Miss Landon,

" L. E. L.," of whom he had said in the " Manufacturer " that she " laid open to the world the
secrets of a heart exquisitely alive to earnest and
clinging affections," and to whom he addresses
verses in the " New England Review " containing
the prophecy : —

" The gifted ones in after years shall worship at thy shrine,
  And Earth's high spirits joy to hold companionship with
    thine."

And the analytic reader would no doubt also find
traces in his work of the influence of his friend
Mrs. Sigourney, whose writing much resembled
that of L. E. L. But some instinct held him to
his experiments in the vein of Mrs. Hemans, the
romantic, narrative, lyric treatment of striking
historical events ; and, wonder of wonders, in the
midst of these juvenile scrawlings suddenly appeared the handiwork of the artist. In the scores
of scores of poems he had written up to 1832
there were only three of any possible value, —
" The Song of the Vermonters," the sole worthy
achievement of his school-days, " The Vaudois
Teacher," and " The Star of Bethlehem." These
last were both printed in 1830 and are both preserved in his collected works ; of both Mrs. Hemans might have been the author. But while
the originality is slight, the growth in skill is
notable. For once the hand is steady and the
outlines clear. In both he had chanced on sub-

jects attractive to Protestants; both dealt with
the spread of the gospel, with that strange re-
modelling of the world through the new message
of the evangels, — a mission profuse in picturesque incident, a romantic as well as a philanthropic mission, which, in its new form, was
firing many of the finest minds in England and
America with religious passion. Both appealed
to the people at large, and "The Vaudois
Teacher," translated into French, became a
household classic among the Waldenses. Both
move swiftly; and in "The Star of Bethlehem,"
in such lines as

> "And what am I, o'er such a land
>   The banner of the Cross to bear?
> Dear Lord, uphold me with Thy hand,
>   Thy strength with human weakness share!"

we hear for an instant the anticipatory note —
the special tone, melody, and manner of his
maturer years.

In brief, we have in these few years the most
pathetic period in Whittier's career. Nurtured
in the veriest nook of the world, and bred a
quietist, he had been flung out into the outer
regions of disillusionment. Love drove him
hither and yon; ambition seized him; he was
pelted, praised, snubbed, satirized; he saw the
seeming hollowness of life; he felt rebellious
despair. And now, broken in health, doubly

disappointed in love, he was thrown back into
the peaceful hillside nook of his boyhood, there
to brood over his part in life until, a year later,
reality conquered fantasy, and he laid hold of
the work that was his and not another's. Meanwhile his art was growing as his intellect developed, nourished by the great underlying currents
of patriotism and religion. Little that he had
written would match the poems contained in
the earliest volume of good American verse, —
the "Miscellaneous Poems Selected from the
United States Literary Gazette" (1826), — that
austere group of verses by Bryant, Percival, and
Longfellow. But in 1832 Percival's best work
was done; Bryant was a lawyer, journalist, and
politician, and was destined never to surpass
those early productions; Longfellow was likely
to be little more than a clever schoolmaster;
Willis was placidly and continually trivial; Poe's
star was scarcely above the horizon. There was
nowhere in America a writer of verse with more
immediate promise than Whittier, and he was a
sick man in the old house at the back of Job's
Hill, disgusted with poetry and planning how he
could best get to Congress.

CHAPTER IV

THE YOUNG ABOLITIONIST

1833–1840

THE crisis in Whittier's life was the moment when, throwing aside his Byronic passion for fame, his selfish zeal for political preferment, he identified himself with the abolitionist movement, then the most forlorn of forlorn hopes. He that loseth his life shall save it: the sacrifice of self, the devotion to a humanitarian end, brought out the nobler side of his genius, and gave him, when he no longer desired it, the fame he once had craved. As he said in later years to a boy seeking counsel, "My lad, if thou wouldst win success, join thyself to some unpopular but noble cause." What it personally meant to Whittier to take this stand, what the direction was which it gave to his verse and his prose, cannot be understood without a careful survey of the movement.

The romantic movement in letters was merely one side of a wave of tender feeling which swept over almost all civilized nations, and which was at its height in America during the second

quarter of the nineteenth century. The rational
movement of the preceding century had led to
theoretical independence and equality among the
whites in the United States. At the same time
it was not to be disputed that the country was far
from unified. The Union had been made up of
various groups of communities, each group abid-
ing by its own laws and customs, and while holding necessary commercial relations with others,
not having any close sympathy with them. This
old tribal or sectional feeling still held firm,
both in New England and in the South, under-
neath the superficies of national feeling, and
not until after the recent Spanish war could the
unification and nationalization of the country be
regarded as reasonably complete. But in spite
of this crude and selfish sectional feeling there
was working throughout the land, and notably
among New Englanders, a marked altruistic
sentiment, a growing pity for the unfortunate or
sinful members of their own or other communities. The same sentiment existed also in England
and Scotland, and may in general be regarded
as a working out into general practice of the
individualistic forces of Puritanism, and as particularly connected with the various dissenting
sects, all of which were marked by a keen and
tender realization of the brotherhood of man.
But the influence of the church must not be

regarded as directly potent in this altruistic development. Indeed, the church, essentially a conservative force when once firmly established, had often to be reformed from within before it would take up these movements for the reformation of the outer world. That is but natural. The movers in any marked social change must be such as are psychologically able readily to form new associations, to group the facts of life in a new way. Men whose brains have this flexibility are rarely the learned or the rich. They are more likely to be simple-minded folk, or even outcasts, who have not been bred into conformity with a fixed pattern of life, who have not learned to regard the world as bound by strict laws. Certainly, not to states or churches or colleges belongs the honor of inaugurating the abolitionist movement. All of these long stood in the way. In the country and in the hearts of simple farmers and mechanics grew the seeds of reform that had been planted by the religious revolt of the seventeenth century, that were nourished by the political revolt of the eighteenth century, and were now brought to blossom by the emotional revolt of the nineteenth century.

This altruistic feeling was oddly compounded of pity and dogmatism. "You unfortunate others who are intemperate or slaves or heathen," it seemed to say, "you are to be pitied; govern-

ment and custom have combined to keep you on
the wrong path; but I have discovered the right
path, and in the face of all opposition, I, though
I stand alone, will put you on it, whether you
wish it or not." And so arose temperance agitators and temperance societies, abolitionists and
abolition societies, missionaries and missionary
societies, and hosts of minor reformers, a perfect
army of pestering people, mad for reconstructing
state and church and society, thrusting their
appeals and their advice in the face of the whole
world. All common sense and common prudence
discountenanced their extreme doctrines. Mostly
poor, such reconstructionists frequently depended
for their support upon the community, subjected
their wives to hardships, and condemned their
children, of whom there was usually no scarcity,
to enter the fierce battle of life without help from
their parents. Thus breaking all the laws of
orderly family growth, and of the upbuilding of
righteousness by regular means, they persisted
that they were chosen of the Lord not to labor
as ordinary men, but to be supported by others
while they were elevating the morals of the
world. On the side of their self-appointed duties
they were by necessity extremists, pressing upon
the world violent reforms, destroying vested
interests, going counter to long-established customs. And yet these men, with their tendency

to shiftlessness, with their bad manners and im-
perfect education, slaves of a new idea, were in
reality what they claimed to be, — the lever by
which civilization was to be hoisted from its old
rut, the purifiers of ancient abuses; and among
them were a few who were the most saintly, the
most noble, and the most far-seeingly logical of
their generation. It was to this motley band of
reformers that Whittier was now to ally himself,
under the special banner of abolitionism. " A just
survey of the whole world can leave little doubt,"
wrote Harriet Martineau, " that the abolitionists
of the United States are the greatest people now
living and moving in it." [1]

In America slavery had been generally condemned by the most advanced thinkers and the
most humane minds. The abolition of slaves,
Jefferson wrote in 1774, is the great object of
our desire. The first step towards that end was
the stopping of importation; but such laws as
were made by Virginia to that effect were vetoed
by the king, and Burke declared that this refusal,
for the sake of gain, to aid the suppression of
this inhuman traffic was one of the causes of the
struggle for independence. In 1787 an ordinance,
voted for even by the Southern delegates, prohibited slavery in the great Northwestern territory,
out of which new states were to be carved. There

[1] *London and Westminster Review,* December, 1838.

was still a strong feeling against the importation
of slaves, but the Carolinas and Georgia, for
economic reasons, persisted in upholding the
practice, and rather than lose their support a
compromise was made, and it was agreed that
importation was not to be prohibited until 1808.
At that time importation into the West Indies
was still allowed by Great Britain, and the attitude of the United States was, on the whole, in
advance of the times. In the last decade of the
eighteenth century, there was much agitation in
favor of abolition, but it was finally determined
that, as Congress was pledged not to stop importation until 1808, it had no authority to interfere
in the affairs of states in favor of emancipation.
When the term of years was reached, and the
importation of slaves was prohibited, it was
generally felt that the question was settled.
Slavery was abandoned in the North, and its
further increase in the South by importation was
stopped; it was expected that it would be prohibited in the new states and would decrease in
the old. The abolition societies were disbanded
and the claims of humanitarianism were satisfied.

But rapid progress in economic conditions
brought about unexpected results. The inven-
tion of the cotton gin, and the enormous profit
to be derived through its use by blacks in regions
where whites could not work, drew several states

into raising almost nothing except cotton, and
turned them away from manufacturing. Slaves
were used up more rapidly in the unfavorable
climates; and as importation was forbidden, it
became profitable to breed them, in favorable
climates, to supply the increasing demand. A distinct group of plantation states was thus formed
and perpetuated, based on an economic basis of
property in man. In these a distinct form of
society grew up, a society rich, cultivated, and
intelligent, but economically reactionary, in that
it rested on a principle of patriarchal control
which, in that special form, the civilized world
was rapidly discarding. It soon became impossible for Southerners to conceive of living under
any other system. Tariff legislation only increased the difference between the Northern and
the Southern systems, and the growing wealth
of the section was an argument for content. In
the South all sensible people deplored slavery;
but how could it be changed? It was apparently
destined that an inferior race should labor for
them in this fashion; any other arrangement
was inconceivable; and they were all naturally
anxious to extend this familiar social organization
into new and contiguous states. On the other
hand, the North, while attached to its own system and anxious to extend it into other states,
was indifferent to slavery in the South. The

North profited by its relations with the South, and hence by slavery. Slavery was an evil, but not one of the North's making, nor one that lay within its legal power to attack. As Daniel Webster, who represented the best opinion of the North, said in his debate with Hayne, "The slavery of the South has always been regarded as a matter of domestic policy left with the states themselves, and with which the federal government had nothing to do. . . . I regard domestic slavery as one of the greatest evils, both moral and political. But whether it be a malady and whether it be curable, and if so, by what means; or, on the other hand, whether it be the *vulnus immedicabile* of the social system, I leave it to those whose right and duty it is to inquire and decide. And this I believe is, and uniformly has been, the sentiment of the North."

But only the part of the North which was bound by the conventions of trade and state and church was wholly indifferent to slavery. More open minds everywhere, and particularly the inhabitants of certain rural districts, knew it to be a gigantic evil; and people who had been brought into connection with European criticism were ashamed of the vital inconsistency between the spirit of liberty contemplated by the theory of American institutions and the sad fact of a civilization that was so largely based on

slavery. Even their uneasy consciences, however, were often lulled to rest by the apparent
activity of the Colonization Society, in which
slave-owners were largely interested, and on
which church and state alike looked with favor.
Its aim was to encourage the emigration to
Africa or Haiti of free blacks, and many hoped
that voluntary emancipation would soon swell
the numbers of these emigrants and decrease
rapidly the slave population.

It was at this juncture that Benjamin Lundy,
a deaf little Quaker, indefatigable in his efforts
to promote colonization, began publishing his
" Genius of Universal Emancipation," and laboring in a very humble way to create a public opinion in the South in favor of some plan
of voluntary emancipation. In 1828 he visited
Boston and tried in vain to get the attention and
support of the clergymen. They turned a deaf
ear and a dull mind to his entreaties, but he was
eagerly listened to by William Lloyd Garrison,
who was determined to give his life to humanitarian reforms. Shortly afterwards Garrison
went to Bennington, Vt., to edit an Adams
paper, in which incidentally he advocated gradual
emancipation for slaves, and he was also interested in the petition of 1829 for emancipation
by the central government of slaves in the District of Columbia. His devotion to this species

of reform grew rapidly, and in 1829 he joined Lundy in Baltimore and became co-editor of the " Genius of Universal Emancipation," bringing into that mild paper the aggressive methods of a political journalist.   He attacked the local slave trade vigorously, and finally, in the absence of his colleague, he roundly berated a Newbury-port shipmaster who took a cargo of slaves from Baltimore to New Orleans, was promptly sued for libel, and as promptly convicted by a Balti-more jury.   Unable to meet the large fine, he lay for some weeks in jail, until released by the payment of it by a New York philanthropist.

Garrison was a man of iron resolve, and pun-ishment only fanned his indignation to white heat.   He returned to Boston and began at once an active propaganda.   He now saw two things plainly : first, the colonization idea was a hin-drance and not a help, and gradual emancipa-tion led nowhere ; second, it was immediate and unconditional emancipation and residence as a freeman on American soil that was the slave's right.   This doctrine, almost absolutely novel at that time, he preached with vehemence, publicly and privately, in the autumn of 1830.   He soon converted to his way of thinking a few humani-tarians, of whom young Unitarian clergymen formed an important part. On January 1, 1831, without capital, and aided only by an old friend,

Knapp, who was a journeyman printer, and a
colored boy, he began to publish the "Liberator,"
which bore the motto, "Our country is the
world — our countrymen are mankind." His
announcement of his purpose said flatly : "Urge
me not to use moderation in a cause like the
present. I am in earnest — I will not equivo-
cate — I will not excuse — I will not retreat a
single inch — AND I WILL BE HEARD."

Garrison and his little band thus boldly ar-
rayed themselves against the hard and fast
opinions of the society surrounding them. Negroes were generally thought to be a happy-go-
lucky race, fairly well off in bondage. The
South bitterly resented any criticism of its social
and economic system. Merchants did not wish
a question raised that shook the foundations of
that system. The church thought slavery a part
of the divine plan of affairs, to be bettered only
by colonization. The ministers did not purpose
to have the public taught its moral duty by any
one not a properly accredited representative of a
religious body. College professors objected to
being instructed in their duty by a young and
obscure journalist. Garrison's idea was naturally thought to be pure fanaticism, and no
modern anarchist is now regarded as more dan-
gerously subversive of sound economic and political doctrine than was he.

Though the dogma of immediate emancipation attracted unusual attention, it did not at first spread rapidly. A little band of a dozen or more had joined with Garrison in forming, in January, 1832, the New England Anti-Slavery Society. The "Liberator" gained a few subscribers, and was as widely circulated as the slender means of the reformers would allow. It preached incessantly that the slaves were held in unlawful bondage, and the implication was that they would be justified in revolting. Garrison was far from encouraging them to do so, and the "Liberator" was not put into the hands of slaves; but when the Nat Turner insurrection of 1831 came, the South naturally connected it with Garrison's propaganda, and was enraged that a Northern state should allow the publication of such a dangerous and seditious sheet. Boston in its turn was enraged that a sister state could have such just cause for reproach against her. North and South alike, people called for the repression by law of the "Liberator."

In 1832 and 1833 the agitation spread more rapidly, increased by the publication in 1832 of Garrison's "Thoughts on African Colonization," and in 1833 by the act of Great Britain in emancipating the slaves in her West Indian colonies. The hatred of the abolitionists was meanwhile growing more bitter, and in 1833, when Miss Prudence Crandall of Canterbury, Conn., attempted to open a school for the education of free negro girls, the whole town rose in arms, treating her with legal severity and personal indignity. It was at this stage of public opinion that two fairly well-known writers, Whittier and Mrs. Lydia Maria Child, made plain their sympathy with the new movement by publishing respectively, in 1833, "Justice and Expediency" and "An Appeal in Favor of that Class of Americans called Africans."

What it meant to come flatly out as an abolitionist at that time should be clearly borne in mind. Men of humane views, North and South, were opposed to slavery, in principle or in practice or in both; but to assert the theory of unconditional emancipation was to promulgate a startling and, to most minds, a frightfully dangerous doctrine. It meant the overthrow of our political and social system: it meant universal suffrage, it meant amalgamation, it meant the civilization of South America and the West Indies. No wonder men stood aghast. Now Whittier was an anti-slavery man by virtue of his Quaker birthright, but so far he had not identified himself with the abolitionists. His reference in the "New England Review" to the establishment of the "Liberator" was kindly but not enthusiastic; he apparently regarded Garrison's propa-

ganda for abolition in just the same light as any
other humanitarian effort, — as that for temperance, for example, — and, ill as he was at
the time, he had taken no share in the formation
of the New England Anti-Slavery Society in
1832. It must not be forgotten, moreover, that
his mind was so set on political preferment, and
he apparently had so clear a chance of representing his district in the next Congress, that he was
not in close communication with his non-political
friends. But an accident brought him again
under Garrison's direct influence. In March,
1833, Garrison, about to sail for England on the
statesmanlike mission of cutting off the powerful
British support given his arch-enemy, the Colonization Society, wrote incidentally to some young
ladies at Haverhill : —

"You excite my curiosity and interest still
more by informing me that my dearly beloved
Whittier is a *friend* and townsman of yours.
Can we not induce him to devote his brilliant
genius more to the advancement of our cause,
and kindred enterprises, and less to the creations
of romance and fancy, and the disturbing incidents of political strife ? " [1]

"You think my influence will prevail with my
dear Whittier more than yours. I think otherwise. If he has not already blotted my name

[1] *William Lloyd Garrison*, i. 331, March 4.

from the tablet of his memory, it is because his magnanimity is superior to neglect. We have had no correspondence whatever, for more than a year, with each other! Does this look like friendship between us? And yet I take the blame all to myself. He is not a debtor to me —I owe him many letters. My only excuse is an almost unconquerable aversion to pen, ink, and paper (as well he knows), and the numerous obligations which rest upon me, growing out of my connection with the cause of emancipation. Pray secure his forgiveness, and tell him that my love to him is as strong as was that of David to Jonathan. Soon I hope to send him a contrite epistle; and I know he will return a generous pardon." [1]

This chance correspondence led Garrison to send to Whittier (March 22, 1833) a letter apologizing for his long silence and urging him to turn his pen to philanthropic and particularly to abolitionist uses.

"I presume you have been busy with your pen — your elastic, vigorous, glowing pen — and are preparing to surprise and delight the public. Study to make your productions as much distinguished for their usefulness as their brilliancy, and you will bless mankind.

"My brother, there are upwards of two million

[1] *William Lloyd Garrison*, i. 331, March 18.

of our countrymen who are doomed to the most horrible servitude which ever cursed our race and blackened the page of history. There are one hundred thousand of their offspring kidnapped annually from their birth. The southern portion of our country is going down to destruction, physically and morally, with a swift descent, carrying other portions with her. This, then, is a time for the philanthropist — any friend of his country, to put forth his energies, in order to let the oppressed go free, and sustain the republic. The cause is worthy of Gabriel — yea, the God of hosts places himself at its head. Whittier, enlist! — Your talents, zeal, influence — all are needed." [1]

Garrison suggested a visit to Haverhill, where Whittier, as he requested, found him a meeting-house in which he could speak on slavery, and on April 3 Garrison wrote to Miss Harriet Minot of the pleasure the trip had given him. "But," he concludes, "pleasant as it is to behold the face of Nature, it has no beauty like the countenance of a beloved friend. Sweet is the song of birds, but sweeter the voices of those we love. To see my dear Whittier once, full of health and manly beauty, was pleasurable indeed." [2]

[1] Manuscript in the possession of the Misses Johnson and Mrs. Woodman.

[2] *William Lloyd Garrison*, i. 332.

The reference to David and Jonathan was not a mere figure of speech. The personal intimacy between the two young men had never been great, but there existed between them a strong bond of friendship. They came from the same district; they had the same humanitarian instincts. Garrison had been the means of awakening Whittier's desire for an education and later of leading him into journalism, and his faith in Whittier's ability had been unfailing. "Our friend Whittier," he wrote in the Bennington "Journal of the Times" in 1828, "seems determined to elicit our best panegyrics, and not ours only, but also those of the public. His genius and situation no more correspond with each other than heaven and earth. But let him not despair. Fortune will come, ere long, ' with both hands full.' " [1] Whittier had induced Clay to move — too late, as it happened — in freeing Garrison from his Baltimore imprisonment, and he had felt for him and his reform the admiration expressed in his verses " To William Lloyd Garrison," published in the Haverhill "Gazette" in November, 1831 : —

> " I love thee with a brother's love,
>   I feel my pulses thrill,
> To mark thy spirit soar above
>   The cloud of human ill.

[1] *William Lloyd Garrison*, i. 115.

My heart hath leaped to answer thine,
    And echo back thy words,
As leaps the warrior's at the shine
    And flash of kindred swords ! "

They were now to work side by side in the abolition movement, and though Garrison was from
first to last its head and front, Whittier also
played an important part. With the same end
in view, they eventually chose widely different
but equally effective means.

Whittier had perhaps already made up his mind
to join the anti-slavery movement before Garrison's brief visit to Haverhill. But that visit must
have strengthened his purpose and hastened the
coming of the sleepless nights which overtook
him when he realized what effect on his political
aspirations such an action would have. "Justice
and Expediency: or, Slavery Considered with a
View to its Rightful and Effectual Remedy,
Abolition," was published in June, 1833, but in
May he wrote to Caleb Cushing, the rising politician of his district, the following letter, characteristic, in the absence of exuberance and in its
mild-spoken craft, of the more manly mood into
which he had now entered : —

"About a fortnight ago, I took up a pamphlet
containing your remarks at the colonization
meeting in Boston. In that frankness which
accords with my ideas of doing to others as I

would be done by, I cannot but say that I deeply regret this publication. So far as literary merit is concerned the speech is worthy of you, but I dissent from your opinions most radically, and so do a great majority of the people in this vicinity. I shall probably send you in a week or two a pamphlet on the subject of slavery, written hastily and under many disadvantages. Most of the facts it contains you are probably already acquainted with. There may be some, however, which have escaped your observation. I beg of you to lend your mind to the investigation of this most momentous question, believing as I do that you can do a great deal for the cause of suffering humanity. I should like to have you make this pamphlet and others recently published on the subject the basis of an article in some of our reviews or magazines. That you will differ from me I know, and shall therefore expect to be handled without gloves, but credit me, my dear sir, I had much rather fall under the *stoccado* of a gentlemanly and scientific swordsman than be bunglingly hewed in pieces like Agag of old under the broadaxe of the Prophet. I have only time again to beg you, whatever may be the result of this trial, to allow yourself to be a candidate still. Sooner or later we must triumph." [1]

[1] Pickard, *Life*, i. 126.

Garrison's "Thoughts on Colonization" had
been aimed directly at the organization for getting free negroes out of the country, which, as
he clearly saw, was the greatest obstacle in the
way of the new movement; Wright's "Sin of
Slavery" was directed to the conscience of the
community; Mrs. Child's "Appeal" was the
successful attempt of a popular writer to place
before the public a large amount of necessary
but miscellaneous information about the negro,
of whose abilities she entertained somewhat
romantic ideas. Whittier's pamphlet, as might
have been expected, was purely and simply a
political tract. In the solitude of his farm he
had been studying Burke and Milton, and the
method of the former and the spirit of the latter had impressed him deeply.[1] His idea was
to make a telling argument in favor of the proposition that abolition was expedient as well as
just. He showed briefly that colonization was
ineffective, and then proceeded to prove as well
as he could, from the results of emancipation in
St. Domingo and elsewhere, that "Historical
facts; the nature of the human mind; the de-
monstrated truths of political economy; the ana-

[1] In old age he declared that his whole life had felt the influence of Milton's writings (Mrs. Fields, *Whittier*, 41) and his
marked copy of Milton's political essays bears witness to the
same fact.

lysis of cause and effect, all concur in establishing: 1. That immediate abolition is a safe and
just and peaceful remedy for evils of the slave
system. 2. That free labor, its necessary consequence, is more productive, and more advan-
tageous to the planter than slave labor." [1]

To the modern reader, with the later history
of Haiti in mind, the argument is anything but
conclusive. It is plea rather than proof. Whittier had not enough evidence at his disposal to
make a telling argument. Yet his attempt, with
all its lack of judicial tone, was on the right
track, and was consonant with his special share in
the abolition movement, — an insistence on the
appeal to reason, a wish to reach the end desired
only by legal means. *Immediate* emancipation,
he said, was merely in contrast with *gradual*
emancipation : —

"Earnestly as I wish it, I do not expect, no
one expects, that the tremendous system of
oppression can be instantaneously overthrown.
The terrible and unrebukable indignation of a
free people has not yet been sufficiently concentrated against it. The friends of abolition have
not forgotten the peculiar organization of our
confederacy, the delicate division of power between the states and the general government.
They see the many obstacles in their pathway;

[1] "Justice and Expediency," in *Prose Works*, iii. 34.

but they know that public opinion can overcome
them all. They ask no aid of physical coercion.
They seek to obtain their object not with the
weapons of violence and blood, but with those
of reason and truth, prayer to God, and entreaty
to man." [1]

Public opinion, expressed through the suffrage, was, then, to be the means of emancipation.
Nothing but a strong, unequivocal expression of
public sentiment was needed. " Let Delaware
begin the work, and Maryland and Virginia
must follow; the example will be contagious;
and the great object of universal emancipation
will be attained."

Whittier's pamphlet attracted immediate attention. He had published five hundred copies
at his own expense, thus sacrificing what must
have been the savings of the whole winter; but
through the kind offices of Lewis Tappan of New
York, it was reprinted as number four, volume
one, of the monthly " Anti-Slavery Reporter,"
five thousand copies of which were distributed,
and it was also printed in the Providence " Journal." The Southern papers resented this new
attempt at interference with their local social
system, and the Richmond " Jeffersonian and
Times " introduced an extract from it with the
statement that it exhibited " in strong colors the

---

[1] " Justice and Expediency," in *Prose Works*, iii. 26.

morbid spirit of false and fanatical philanthropy which is at work in the Northern states, and, to some extent, in the South." Whittier's reply, "The Abolitionists: Their Sentiments and Objects,"[1] published in the Haverhill "Gazette," was almost as long as the original pamphlet, and was in most respects cautious and conciliatory. He was merely "a humble son of New England, — a tiller of her rugged soil," and it mattered little personally whether words of praise or opprobrium reached him from beyond the narrow limits of his immediate neighborhood. His remarks were, at that busy season of the year, written hastily and in the brief intervals of labor. But he must defend his cause from the charge of fanaticism, and he went on to review the ground, pointing out the traditional Virginian desire for emancipation, the advantage to her in emancipation, and the reason why the rest of the Union was vitally concerned in her action, and was therefore protecting its own rights rather than needlessly interfering in the affairs of others.

An important convert, Whittier was now fully committed to the movement, and in December of the same year, 1833, he assisted as one of the delegates from Massachusetts in the solemn founding, in Philadelphia, of the American Anti-

[1] Reprinted in *Prose Works*, iii. 58.

Slavery Society. "I set a higher value on my name as appended to the Anti-Slavery Declaration of 1833," he used afterwards to say, "than on the title-page of any book." It was indeed an honor and a privilege. It confirmed his dedication to a noble cause, and set him apart, once and for all, from the selfish individualism of the politician.

The men with whom he was now allied, and their fervor of conviction, he himself best described in 1874, in his remarkably vivid "Anti-Slavery Convention of 1833 : " [1] —

"Looking over the assembly, I noticed that it was mainly composed of comparatively young men, some in middle age, and a few beyond that period. They were nearly all plainly dressed, with a view to comfort rather than elegance. Many of the faces turned towards me wore a look of expectancy and suppressed enthusiasm. All had the earnestness which might be expected of men engaged in an enterprise beset with difficulty and perhaps with peril. The fine intellectual head of Garrison, prematurely bald, was conspicuous. The sunny-faced young man at his side, in whom all the beatitudes seemed to find expression, was Samuel J. May, mingling in his veins the best blood of the Sewalls and Quincys, — a man so exceptionally pure and large-hearted,

[1] *Prose Works*, iii. 171.

so genial, tender, and loving, that he could be
faithful to truth and duty without making an
enemy. . . . That tall, gaunt, swarthy man,
erect, eagle-faced, upon whose somewhat martial
figure the Quaker coat seemed a little out of
place, was Lindley Coates, known in all eastern
Pennsylvania as a stern enemy of slavery. That
slight, eager man, intensely alive in every feature and gesture, was Thomas Shipley, who for
thirty years had been the protector of the free
colored people of Philadelphia, and whose name
was whispered reverently in the slave cabins of
Maryland as the friend of the black man, one
of a class peculiar to old Quakerism, who in
doing what they felt to be duty and walking as
the Light within guided them knew no fear and
shrank from no sacrifice. Braver men the world
has not known. Beside him, differing in creed,
but united with him in works of love and charity,
sat Thomas Whitson, of the Hicksite school of
Friends, fresh from his farm in Lancaster
County, dressed in plainest homespun, his tall
form surmounted by a shock of unkempt hair,
the odd obliquity of his vision contrasting
strongly with the clearness and directness of his
spiritual insight. Elizur Wright, the young
professor of a Western college, who had lost his
place by his bold advocacy of freedom, with a
look of sharp concentration in keeping with an

intellect keen as a Damascus blade, closely
watched the proceedings through his spectacles,
opening his mouth only to speak directly to the
purpose. . . . Vermont sent down from her
mountains Orson S. Murray, a man terribly in
earnest, with a zeal that bordered on fanaticism,
and who was none the more genial for the mob
violence to which he had been subjected. In
front of me, awakening pleasant associations of
the old homestead in Merrimac valley, sat my
first school-teacher, Joshua Coffin, the learned
and worthy antiquarian and historian of Newbury. A few spectators, mostly of the Hicksite
division of Friends, were present, in broad brims
and plain bonnets, among them Esther Moore
and Lucretia Mott.

"The reading of the paper [the declaration
of principles] was followed by a discussion which
lasted several hours. A member of the Society
of Friends moved its immediate adoption. 'We
have,' he said, 'all given it our assent: every
heart here responds to it. It is a doctrine
of Friends that these strong and deep impressions should be heeded.' The convention, nevertheless, deemed it important to go over the
declaration carefully, paragraph by paragraph.
During the discussion one of the spectators asked
leave to say a few words. A beautiful and
graceful woman in the prime of life, with a face

beneath her plain cap as finely intellectual as that of Madame Roland, offered some wise and valuable suggestions in a clear, sweet voice, the charm of which I have never forgotten. It was Lucretia Mott of Philadelphia. The president courteously thanked her, and encouraged her to take a part in the discussion. On the morning of the last day of our session the declaration, with its few verbal amendments, carefully engrossed on parchment, was brought before the convention. Samuel J. May rose to read it for the last time. His sweet, persuasive voice faltered with the intensity of his emotions as he repeated the solemn pledges of the concluding paragraphs. After a season of silence, David Thurston of Maine rose as his name was called by one of the secretaries, and affixed his name to the document. One after another passed up to the platform, signed, and retired in silence. All felt the deep responsibility of the occasion: the shadow and forecast of a lifelong struggle rested upon every countenance."

The abolitionists now grew in numbers and strength with surprising rapidity. Every man's hand had at first been raised against them. Presidents, governors, and mayors treated them as brawling disturbers of the national peace. The church charged them with disrespect for the divinely established order of the world. Citi-

zens — good and bad, rich and poor — joined
to mob them. The popular fury reached its
height in 1835 and 1836. When Garrison
visited England in 1833 he had not only broken
the back of the interest felt there for the absurd
colonization scheme, but had roused the enthusiasm of George Thompson, an eloquent speaker
who had done much to bring about the English
emancipation laws and who was now willing to
devote himself to a corresponding work in America. When he arrived, in 1834, Americans were
furious. They were angry with Garrison for
having betrayed his country by insisting on her
shame in his English addresses, but their rage
at being taught their duty by a foreigner was
naturally boundless. An Englishman, one of
the nation against whom we fought for freedom,
teach *us* what freedom is! Rewards were said
to have been offered for his life. Certainly he
was in many places greeted with abuse and violence, and it was on his account that the famous
" broadcloth " riot of 1835 took place, in which
he was roughly treated by a mob that included
" many gentlemen of property and standing."

But events moved so rapidly, and the natural
dislike for a troublesome reform was so far
counteracted by that passion for free speech
which is the basic virtue of New Englanders,
that by 1837 the worst of popular opposition

was past; and in the reaction of the public mind that followed the Lovejoy murder a Faneuil Hall meeting was held in which the abolitionists took almost the place of honor. By this time, too, they had many auxiliary societies and many important adherents. Men of letters, to be sure, were still lacking. Longfellow was buried in his pleasant books; Hawthorne was a recluse; Lowell was in his callow years, and had satirized the abolitionists in his class-day poem; Emerson, following lines of more abstract thought, was suspicious of mundane reformers. But constant additions were being made to the ranks of the party; and when in 1836 the "great" Dr. Channing brought out his carefully considered book against slavery, — weak and faltering though it was, and at its best merely a repetition of what the abolitionists had been saying since 1831, — the ice of conservative gentility was first broken.

Just when the horizon was thus clearing for the abolitionists, it was darkened by dissensions in the midst of their own body, — dissensions which were accompanied by bitterness and heated dispute at the time, and which were thought to be a source of weakness, but which, after the lapse of more than half a century, we now recognize as merely divisions due to natural differences of motive and policy.

Garrison was the last of the great Puritan prophets. His scheme of thought and action was exclusively moral and religious. He advocated many reforms. He upheld the equal rights of women; he held some of the vague religious doctrines of the perfectionists; he looked confidently towards a millennium of righteousness; he was a non-combatant; he regarded earthly and civic governments as temporary evils without divine sanction; he deprecated the extreme insistence of the church on such minor matters as the keeping of the Sabbath. The greatest moral force of his time, he was rigorous in his condemnation of all faltering and compromise, of all alliance with evil. He depended for the attainment of his aims on the moral regeneration of man. Around him as their leader, and the " Liberator " as their standard, gathered a group of devoted men and women, — Wendell Phillips, Edmund Quincy, Mrs. Chapman, and Mrs. Child, — " the Boston clique," who held fast to this main doctrine of emancipation through the moral and religious education of the people. As time went on, they advocated disunion, and explicitly disavowed allegiance to a government that permitted slavery.

Whittier, on the other hand, showed his Quaker training. His family and his sect had been dissenters, reformers, and " come-outers " for centuries, and he took things more quietly and more shrewdly. The world was not all to be reformed at once. One thing at a time. The main end to be secured at that moment was abolition; all other reforms, about which there might be difference of opinion, must be subordinated to it. He acknowledged Garrison as the originator of the movement and its greatest force, but he deplored his terrible earnestness of utterance, which permanently alienated his opponents; his tendency to obscure the main issue by taking up minor reforms; his refusal to entertain the idea of political coalition. In this general attitude he was in accordance with the more common feeling in New York State and city and in Philadelphia, and in particular with his colleagues, Elizur Wright, Theodore B. Stanton, and Gerrit Smith.

This difference of opinions as to ways and means led eventually to a fairly sharp division of abolitionists into two classes — the old organization or Garrisonians, and the new organization. The first split, queerly enough, came on the right or advisability of women's taking a prominent or official part in abolitionist meetings. Garrison insisted that they should stand on the same footing as men and encouraged their speaking. In this he seemed to be clearly on the right side, for many of the important abolitionists were women. But the public was not yet accustomed to the idea of women's concerning themselves in matters of state, and Whittier and his friends were anxious that obloquy should not fall on the cause on this account. As for himself, he was not unaccustomed, through Quaker custom, to the equality of the sexes in important matters; and though he thought it better that women should confine themselves mainly to domestic affairs and avoid undue publicity, his objection was largely the prudent one of a desire not to give offense. He would have had abolitionism win its way, unencumbered, to the hearts of the people. When, therefore, in 1837 the General Association of Orthodox Congregational churches in Massachusetts published a Pastoral Letter, claiming for the parish minister the exclusive right of determining what moral teachings should be addressed to the people of his town, and singling out for censure the practice of lecturing by women, Whittier, though he satirized the clerical position in spirited verses, was inclined to think that his predictions had been justified. Indeed, when the New England Anti-Slavery Society and the American Anti-Slavery Society adopted Garrison's views on the subject of women, and held more rigidly aloof from concerted political action, he joined with those who preferred to cut loose from Garrison's influence and direction and to form an organization of their own. By 1839 a considerable body in central New York, of whom Stanton was chief, favored the formation of a political anti-slavery party. That year saw the establishment of a new paper in Boston, the " Massachusetts Abolitionist," which was the organ of the new Massachusetts Abolitionist Society, and the next saw the formation of a third political party through a convention held at Albany. In the same year the American Anti-Slavery Society, the old organization, disapproved political action and approved women's rights, insisting on sending women as delegates to the World's Anti-Slavery Convention in London.

With the main steps in this political and philanthropic movement clearly in mind, we may now turn to Whittier's part in it, and to his more individual life, if he can be said to have had an individuality at all in a period when body and soul alike had no inspiration and no duty save that of devotion to a cause.

The change back to the old soil and the home life gave him strength again. The tone of complaint and despair disappeared from his letters; the selfish note of purely personal ambition vanished. Though frequently prostrated by illness, it was clear that his health was essentially better while he lived on the farm and as a farmer. To a friend he wrote in 1833 that he was as busy

with his farm as a beaver building his dam and
that the blues had left him.   It was a life of severe economy, of meagre results, but it kept the
brain clear for his great purpose, and left him the
long evenings free for his writing ; and it is pleasant to think of this handsome young Quaker,
with his flashing eyes and military bearing, driving "his team in the autumn to Rocks Bridge,
which is at the head of tidewater in the Merrimac,
where the coasting vessels from Maine then came,
carrying apples and vegetables to exchange for
salt fish to eke out the winter stores." [1]

But it was only by heroic endeavor that he
could serve his cause.   On February 25, 1834,
he writes thus to Elizur Wright, then secretary
of the American Anti-Slavery Society, explaining his policy as a free lance : —

"Situated as I am, I can at present do but
little.   I cannot as yet accuse myself of neglecting any opportunity for the dissemination of
truth on the great subject of slavery.   The
clergy in this vicinity are rapidly taking side
with us.   There is another class which might, I
think, be easily moved.   I allude to that class
of politicians or civilians whose sphere of influence is limited to their town or county.   These
can take hold of our cause without essentially
endangering their popularity, and through them

[1] F. H. Underwood, *John Greenleaf Whittier*, 137.

the higher classes of our statesmen may be reached. I have some influence with this class. My exertions as a political writer for the last four years have gained me a large number of political friends. The columns of all the leading newspapers are open to me. With many of the editors I am on terms of intimate personal acquaintance. All know me as a quondam brother, as a political friend or opponent. Now if I were at leisure to reply to such misrepresentations and charges as occasionally appear in these papers, to distribute pamphlets and papers, to visit personally gentlemen in my vicinity and engage their coöperation, and finally to combine the anti-slavery feeling upon some definite and practical object, such, for instance, as the election of members of the state legislature, who will bring forward and sustain resolutions instructing our congressional delegation to urge the abolition of slavery in the District of Columbia,— I have no doubt I could do good and efficient service.

"But I have really little leisure for such exertions. In the first place, my brother and myself are almost constantly engaged in the affairs of our small farm, which does not yield profit enough to enable us to hire labor; and I am obliged to occupy my evenings and other leisure time in writing occasional literary articles for the 'New England Magazine,' for which I am paid. Besides this, I have felt myself under the necessity of applying myself to the study of constitutional law, political economy, etc. Whatever I have written on the subject of slavery has been by an effort of extra exertion, and under circumstances of haste and constant interruption.

"Now, if the Executive Committee of the American Anti-Slavery Society could assure me for the term of six months the sum of $150, I should be able to bend all the energies which God has given me to the great work before us; and I fully believe that at the end of that time we shall be able to lend both moral and pecuniary strength to the National Society. I have specified that sum as the smallest which could possibly meet my expenses, as I should be compelled to travel considerably from home, and owing to the consequent interruption of my labor on the farm, I should be under the necessity of hiring a person to supply my place.

"I have been induced to make this proposal from a sincere desire of aiding in the advancement of a righteous cause. I have recently had an offer, highly favorable in a pecuniary point of view, to take charge of a political newspaper; but should I accept it, my mouth would be closed on the subject nearest my heart." [1]

[1] S. T. Pickard, *Whittier as a Politician* (Boston, 1900), 47.

The period of return to mother earth was only just sufficient to gain strength and courage. In 1835 he was a member of the Massachusetts legislature, and he was reëlected for 1836 ; but his new-found health was still precarious, and he had learned that long days of regular labor were never more to lie in his power. He could accomplish much, but it must be in his own way, at his own hours. And so he turned to less rigid duties, to service of many sorts in behalf of his cause, which we must now describe.

These services were sometimes of a kind that demanded physical as well as moral courage. While George Thompson was lecturing in New England, Whittier secreted him for a fortnight at his house from mob violence, and afterwards shared with him the perils then attendant upon free speech on the subject of abolition in a New England city. The incident has been vividly described by Whittier's cousin, Mrs. Cartland : —

. . . " Thinking themselves secure because personally unknown, the two friends drove to Plymouth, N. H., to visit Nathaniel P. Rogers, a prominent abolitionist. On their way they stopped for the night in Concord, at the house of George Kent, who was a brother-in-law of Rogers. After they had gone on their way, Kent attempted to make preparations for an anti-slavery meeting to be held when they should return. There was furious excitement, and neither church, chapel, nor hall could be hired for the purpose. On their arrival Whittier walked out with a friend in the twilight, leaving Thompson in the house, and soon found himself and friend surrounded by a mob of several hundred persons, who assailed them with stones and bruised them somewhat severely. They took refuge in the house of Colonel Kent, who, though not an abolitionist, protected them and baffled the mob. From thence Whittier made his way with some difficulty to George Kent's, where Thompson was. The mob soon surrounded the house and demanded that Thompson and 'the Quaker' should be given up. Through a clever stratagem the mob was decoyed away for a while, but soon discovering the trick, it returned, reinforced with muskets and a cannon, and threatened to blow up the house if the abolitionists were not surrendered.

"A small company of anti-slavery men and women had met that evening at George Kent's, among whom were two nieces of Daniel Webster, daughters of his brother Ezekiel. All agreed that the lives of Whittier and Thompson were in danger, and advised that an effort should be made to escape. The mob filled the street, a short distance below the gate leading to Kent's

house. A horse was quietly harnessed in the
stable, and was led out with the vehicle under
the shadow of the house, where Whittier and
Thompson stood ready. It was bright moon-
light, and they could see the gun-barrels gleam-
ing in the street below them. The gate was
suddenly opened, the horse was started at a furious gallop, and the two friends drove off amidst
the yells and shots of the infuriated crowd.
They left the city by the way of Hookset Bridge,
the other avenues being guarded, and hurried in
the direction of Haverhill. In the morning they
stopped to refresh themselves and their tired
horse. While at breakfast they found that 'ill
news travels fast,' and gets worse as it goes;
for the landlord told them that there had been
an abolition meeting at Haverhill the night before, and that George Thompson, the Englishman, and a young Quaker named Whittier, who
had brought him, were both so roughly handled
that they would never wish to talk abolition
again. When the guests were about to leave,
Whittier, just as he was stepping into the car-
riage, said to the landlord, ' My name is Whittier,
and this is George Thompson.' The man opened
his eyes and mouth with wonder as they drove
away." [1]

But, as a rule, Whittier's life was less full

[1] F. H. Underwood, *Whittier*, 116.

of excitement. He acted in his district as an
agent of the New England Anti-Slavery Society.
In 1836 he was again for some time editor
of the Haverhill "Gazette." In 1837 he was
successively in Harrisburg, Penn., at an anti-
slavery state convention; in Boston, engaged in
lobbying an important measure through the
legislature; and in New York as one of the
secretaries of the American Anti-Slavery Society. In the last city he spent several months,
occupying an office in which James G. Birney,
Theodore D. Weld, Elizur Wright, and others
had desks. Together they edited the "Emancipator" and the "Anti-Slavery Reporter," wrote
appeals to public men, distributed petitions,
wrote tracts, and helped fugitive slaves on the
"underground railroad." He boarded in Brooklyn, where he had a pleasant circle of friends,
and he naturally saw much of his ardent young
associates in reform. His eagerness kept pace
with theirs, and it is related that on one evening
Mr. Weld and he were so engrossed in discussion
that it was nearly daybreak before they parted.
In March, 1838, he again changed his quarters,
assuming charge of the new "Pennsylvania
Freeman," an abolitionist organ published in
Philadelphia, in continuation of the "National
Enquirer," of which the aged Benjamin Lundy
had just resigned the control. Philadelphia was

undergoing its period of mob rule. In May, at the close of the dedication exercises of Pennsylvania Hall, a handsome building devoted to the purposes of the cause, it was seized, sacked, and burned by the citizens, with the connivance of the city authorities. Whittier had his office in this building, and, disguised in a wig and a long white overcoat, he mingled with the mob and succeeded in saving some of his effects. Fortunately the printing offices were not in the building, and the paper continued to appear as usual. Whittier found old friends and new in Philadelphia, and as in New York led a more active life than was permitted to him later. He remained until October, breaking his editorial duties by short journeys in the service of the cause. Then came a few months at home for recuperation, for his strength was again breaking, though he still continued as editor. In April, 1839, he returned to Philadelphia; in June he attended the national political anti-slavery convention in Albany, and in January, 1840, visited Washington, where the great debate on the right of petition was then going on. But in February he was forced by alarming illness to give up his work again, this time virtually forever. His heart was seriously affected, and it was only in the quiet surroundings of his native district, and in the calm old life, that he was

master of what little strength remained to him.
And thus ended the second flight into the outer
world, the second attempt to meet face to face
the great forces of the passionate city centres,
closing like the first in physical defeat.

Meantime the old farm had in 1836 been
given up. Whittier's brother was married and
gone. Whittier himself was unequal to the
management, and the toil and trouble were dis-
proportionate to the meagre returns. After
nearly two centuries of occupancy, therefore,
the land passed into the hands of strangers, and
a pleasant little house was bought on Friend
Street, in the delightful manufacturing village
of Amesbury, which lies a few miles to the east-
ward, where near the sea the boisterous Powow
dashes into the Merrimac. The sunshiny house,
with its pretty garden, stood close by the
Friends' meeting-house, which the Whittiers had
always attended while they lived on the farm,
and the removal was to a community so kindred
that it could scarcely have seemed a radical
change.

It was a strange band of workers with whom
Whittier had been brought into contact in these
years of lobbying and pamphleteering and journalism. In his Hartford sojourn he had seen
something of "worldly" life, of much that was

opposite in tendency to his quietist training; and the glimpse, though it tended to unsettle his mind, was good for him, as it was good for him to imagine himself in love with a woman of another creed and another social circle. Such associations, disquieting at first, would have eventually added to his natural breadth and toleration of mind, led him to know the world better, given his verse a richness which it never attained. But with his illness, the giving up of his political ambition, and his devotion to what seemed a futile cause, the bounds of his acquaintance were again straitened. He knew only reformers, and for twenty years or more after his return to Amesbury there is scarcely to be found among his new friends a single person from the greater outer world, save such as were enlisted in his own reform or in some kindred one. These reformers were in many ways the pick of the nation, men and women with brains capable of conceiving a new order of things, and wills strong enough to try to bend the hard world itself to their purpose. Their energy was tremendous, but they lived in the future, neglecting the present, sacrificing even the innocent delights of life in their almost hypnotic devotion to a fixed idea. After reading many of their biographies, I may perhaps single out this passage, from the work of a dispassionate observer, as most characteristic of the temper and mood of the men and women in Boston, New York, and Philadelphia with whom Whittier was brought into close contact : —

"Angelina E. Grimké was married, in the spring of 1838, to Theodore D. Weld, one of the forty seceders from Lane Seminary. The devotion of these ladies to the cause they have espoused is a devotion for life. They give their all to it, — not only their time and labor, not only their slave property, but all their resources. They are now living on the Hudson, about ten miles from New York, thinking the bare support of life enough, since it is sufficient for their object. They have no servant, and they have long given up meat, tea, and coffee. The saving of time is as much an object with them in this as economy of money. Their office is to collect and publish evidence (for which their former experience as slaveholders fits them) relating to the whole system of slavery. They are thus pretty constantly employed in writing. The family sit at their desks till within five minutes of the dinner or supper hour. One of the ladies goes down to prepare the table, and rings the bell as the hour strikes, when the rest descend to their cheerful meal, thus easily prepared. It is thought probable that, without such a change in their mode of living, persons who had been

brought up in the climate, and amidst the lux-
urious indulgences of the Southern states, would
have soon sunk under the toils and excitements
which these ladies have sustained, — thus far,
thank God! without injury to the health of body
or mind." [1]

Such exalted altruism makes saints and
martyrs, and we are grateful for it; but it also
makes a multitude of eccentric, ill-balanced
individuals, who are of little real and lasting
service to the community; and if from this band
of enthusiasts and from their common cause
Whittier drew the fervor and intensity of his
verse in this period, we must notice that from
the same source came its narrow range, its lack
of wide human sympathy, its æsthetic poverty.
The reformer was killing the poet. Yet in these
years of earnest companionship with disinterested
enthusiasts we find traces of friendships with
women standing just outside the abolitionist circles — with Miss Elizabeth Lloyd, Jr., the author of "Milton on his Blindness," to whom there
attached, in the hearts of the Quaker girls of
Philadelphia, "a special glamour because she
was understood to be one of the few with whom
Whittier was really on terms of warm personal
friendship, outside of his firm and faithful com-

[1] Harriet Martineau, "The Martyr Age of the United
States," *London and Westminster Review*, December, 1838.

radeship with his anti-slavery friends;"[1] and with Miss Lucy Hooper, a young author of much sentimental verse, a native of Newburyport, who was living in Brooklyn, and to whom he was thought at one time to be engaged. Such traces of real human feeling show that his old suscepti- bility to feminine charm was not destroyed even by his humanitarian passions.

During this period of origins, Whittier was in three ways of material assistance to the cause he espoused, — as a politician, as a journalist, and as a poet.

It is doubtful whether Whittier's health would have stood the strain of a political career, for which he was in many ways admirably fitted. His one year of service in the Massachusetts legislature broke him down, and though he was reëlected he could not serve. But while not again holding office, he was of great service in political matters. He knew the leading men in the local and national machines, and was in frequent correspondence with them ; and he used the fact that anti-slavery men held the balance of power in his district to pledge Caleb Cushing to action in their behalf in order to secure elec- tion in 1834 and 1836.

[1] Reminiscences of Miss Susan E. Dickinson, in Pickard's *Life*, i. 216.

"I am disappointed," he wrote to Cushing from Newburyport, in 1834, "in not seeing thee at this place and this time, as I called to apprise thee of the fact that at our meeting of the Essex County Anti-Slavery Society yesterday at Danvers, it was unanimously agreed upon to write letters to the candidates for Congress and state legislature on the subject of slavery and of their views of action in Congress and in the legislature upon it. Until after the passage of this resolution I did not reflect that it would embrace thyself and Osgood [his Democratic opponent], as we were thinking of Saltonstall and Rantoul [in the other Essex district]. As it is, however, I hope thee will favor the Society with an explicit answer, as the one hundred and twenty delegates present pledged themselves to vote for no man of any party who was not in favor of abolition in the District of Columbia. I heard, too, from a gentleman in the meeting that two or three hundred of the legal voters of Lowell have pledged themselves to this effect." [1]

Cushing, once elected, held to his word, and regularly presented the abolitionist petitions for doing away with slavery in the District of Columbia, and upheld Adams in his opposition to gag-rule. In 1838, while Whittier was in Philadelphia, Cushing tried to avoid pledging himself

[1] Pickard, *Life*, i. 173.

again, but Whittier returned in season to take
the management of affairs into his own hands.
The result is best described by Mr. Pickard : [1]—

"Cushing declined to pledge himself to spe-
cific measures, saying, 'I cling to my personal
independence as the choicest and richest of all
possessions. I will take my place in Congress
as a freeman or not at all, pledged only to Truth,
Liberty, and the Constitution, with no terror before my eyes but the terror to do wrong. Thus,
or not at all, will I reascend the giant stairs of
the Capitol.' Whittier was determined to get
a more explicit pledge or prevent his election.
At his suggestion, his friend Henry B. Stanton
read Cushing's letter and commented upon it in
a humorous and caustic way, and the convention adjourned without any action in his favor.
Cushing, who was anxious to secure the Liberty vote, was in a corner of the gallery while
his communication was being criticised. In the
evening he met Whittier at the hotel, and expressed his chagrin at the reception given his
careful letter. He said, 'What shall I do?'
Whittier replied, 'Thee cannot expect the votes
of our people, unless thee speaks more plainly.'
'But how can I do that now?' said Cushing.
Whittier suggested, 'Write a short letter to me,
and do not hide thy meaning under many words.'

[1] *Life*, i. 181.

Cushing did not feel like doing it, but said at length, ' Let me see you in the morning.' Whittier was to leave for home by stage quite early, and promised to call for Cushing. He found the anxious statesman half dressed and waiting for him. He had decided to sign any letter that Whittier would write. Whittier thereupon wrote the short letter that follows, which Cushing copied and signed, and it was sent to all parts of the Essex district by special messengers: —

SALEM, November 8, 1838.

MY DEAR SIR,— I should regret to have any doubt remain on your mind as to the import of those points of my letter which are referred to by you. In respect to the District of Columbia, I am in favor of the abolition of slavery and the slave trade therein, by the earliest practicable legislation of Congress, regard being had for the just rights of all classes of the citizens, and I intended to be so understood.

In the concluding part of the letter, I stated that I felt bound to withhold stipulation in detail, as to my future course in Congress. But I did not design it to be understood that I entertained any desire or disposition to change my course in regard to the subjects embraced in the letter; but, on the contrary, being resolved to continue to maintain on all suitable occasions, as I have

heretofore done, the principles and spirit of the
resolves of the legislature of Massachusetts, ap-
pertaining to the right of petition, and to slavery
and the slave trade, in their various relations.

I am, very faithfully, yours,

CALEB CUSHING.

To JOHN G. WHITTIER, Esq.

In 1840 Cushing avoided the pledge and
managed to secure election.   But in 1841, when
the Whigs came into power, and he was anxious
to become Secretary of the Treasury, Whittier
took pains to republish the letter of 1838, which
identified him to some extent with the abolitionists, and it is believed that this was instrumental
in procuring his defeat in the Senate, where the
nomination was three times rejected.   Whittier's
object was not the gratification of spite, but a
conviction that Cushing was a dangerous man to
hold office.

In many other ways Whittier thus helped to
forward the propaganda.   Shrewd and intelligent, an excellent judge of affairs, and a master
of the ins and outs of political intrigue, he was
for years almost the only one of the abolitionists
bent on gaining an inch here and an inch there
in a strictly practical fashion.   Moral action
apart from political action he thought an absurd-
ity.   With a genius for coalition and the art of

playing on the hopes and fears of politicians, he was a familiar figure in the lobby of the Massachusetts legislature, and in 1837 took an active part in the campaign which induced that body, anything but abolitionist at heart, to move directly in the interests of abolitionists by censuring Van Buren's lordly message calling for a cessation of anti-slavery discussion. In no form of action, however, did he show himself more astute than in the clever and earnest letters he wrote to political leaders, explaining to them why it would be to their advantage, and not out of accord with the fundamental principles of their party, to further the abolitionist movement in one way or another.

It was in this politic fashion that he addressed Henry Clay, who had been the idol of his youthful ambitions : [1] —

NEW YORK, 5th, 6th month, 1837,
143 Nassau Street.

HON. H. CLAY, — I make no apology for addressing thee on the subject of human rights. A Republican,— a steady and consistent friend of human liberty, thou canst not be indifferent to the condition of more than two millions of our fellow countrymen, deprived of all the rights,

[1] Copy in the possession of the Misses Johnson and Mrs. Woodman.

and shut out from all the glorious privileges and immunities of American citizens. Thou hast indeed spoken freely on this subject — and in a manner worthy of the advocate of universal liberty. According to thy own emphatic declaration, " SLAVERY IS ALL WRONG."

Thou hast, I doubt not, heard and read much against the abolitionists of the North and West. I trust, however, that thy discriminating mind has been able to perceive that much that has been urged against us is and must be *false* in the nature of things. But I would ask thee to weigh the testimony of such men as Wm. E. Channing and Daniel Webster in regard to the character of the abolitionists. We are *not* the enemies of the slaveholder: and how would our hearts go out to that man who, himself a slaveholder, should throw off the shackles of a corrupt public opinion, shake from him the prejudices of education, despise the suggestions of avarice, crucify the lust of power, and stand forth the fearless and eloquent advocate of the rights of the *colored American!* How many prayers from the closet and around the fireside of the free farmers of New England would arise for his welfare!

The subject is fast becoming the all-engrossing one. Already our societies have increased to 1100,— having more than doubled during the

past year. Almost every mail brings us accounts
of the formation of new societies. In Massachusetts, the great mass is becoming abolition-
ized, and men of both political parties, and of
all religious creeds, unite as upon common
ground. In this state the undercurrent of abolitionism is acquiring tremendous strength. This
question, too, is taken hold of upon *religious*
grounds. It is the conscience — the soul— the
deep religious principle of the North that is
speaking out on this subject. Prayerful men
and women consider the utterance of their testimony against Slavery as a solemn and imperative
duty. And will a cause, thus baptized in prayer,
and associated with the holiest emotions of the
soul, and the best feelings of humanity, fail of
its great object? Believe it not. I will do thee
the justice to believe that thou wouldst not wish
it to fail.

There is one subject upon which I feel a deep
interest. It is the subject of Texas, and its
annexation to the United States. God grant
that my fears may not be realized, but I confess that I have little hope of anything else than
such an annexation. I trust that *thy* voice will
be raised against it.

The Society of Friends as a body feel deeply
on this subject. They would be glad to entrust
some petitions or remonstrances against the

annexation of Texas to thy care could they be assured that thou wouldst sustain the petitions. I should be pleased to have a line from thee on the subject as early as may suit thy convenience.

With respect and esteem,

Thy friend,

JOHN G. WHITTIER.

Clay replied with equal skill:[1]—

(*Private*)

ASHLAND, 22d July, 1837.

DEAR SIR,—I duly received your favor of the 5th inst. and hope you will excuse me for writing very briefly on the several subjects of which it treats. I certainly do, as you suppose, feel great concern in regard to the condition of the African portion of our population. I have so often expressed my sentiments, in respect to slavery, that it is not necessary now to repeat them. Without looking to the religious aspect of the question, all my reflections have satisfied me that it is unjust, and injurious both to the master and slave.

But whilst I say this, candor obliges me to express my deep regret that the abolitionists of the North have deemed it their duty to agitate the question of immediate emancipation. I

[1] Manuscript in the possession of the Misses Johnson and Mrs. Woodman.

will not impute to them bad motives, nor stop
to entertain and discuss the question. But I
must say that I think that their proceedings are
highly injurious to the slave himself, to the
master, and to the harmony of the Union. I
believe that, instead of accelerating, they will
retard abolition, and, in the mean time, will
check the measures of benevolence and amelio-
ration. This, no doubt, was not intended, but it
is nevertheless absolutely certain.

I am not aware that the annexation of Texas
to the U. S. will ever become a question for
general consideration. I learn that the desire
of becoming a part of the U. S. is weakening
in Texas. Should the question arise, it will be
necessary to weigh, with great deliberation, all
the probable consequences both of admission and
exclusion. Slavery is only one of many consid-
erations that will come up. I do not think that
the question should be decided *exclusively* by
that. Should there be a decided opposition by
a large portion of the U. S. to the admission
of Texas into our national family, that fact
ought to have great, if not conclusive, influence
in the determination of the question.

I think those gentlemen of the South have
been unwise who have expressed a wish for the
incorporation of Texas *in order to strengthen
the slave interest ;* and I should think it also

unwise in gentlemen of the North to avow the opposite ground as motive for action.

As for myself, I shall reserve my judgment for all the lights of which I can avail myself when the proposition of annexation shall be made, if it ever be made. It may become a matter of serious enquiry whether the spread of slavery and the introduction of slaves from foreign countries may not be more successfully prevented by taking Texas in the Union than by keeping her out of it.

I am with high respect,

Your obt. servt.

H. CLAY.

As a further illustration of Whittier's political correspondence, I am able to present, through the kindness of Mr. Charles Francis Adams, the following letters to John Quincy Adams, whom he revered as the ideal exponent of moral reform through political means : —

PHILADELPHIA, 23rd 1st mo., 1837.

HON. J. Q. ADAMS, — A citizen of Massachusetts, I feel free to address thee a line in reference to the great question of Slavery as now agitated in this country. In common with thousands of the sons of the " good Bay State," I have felt under peculiar obligations to thyself as the unflinching and uncompromising defender of our right of petition, and as the inflexible opponent of the baneful system of Slavery. In the name of thousands of thy fellow citizens I thank thee. I rejoice to know that whoever else may prove faithless to the Pilgrim Spirit of New England Freedom in the Halls of Congress, the son of John Adams will never be found " basely bowing the knee to the dark Spirit of Slavery."

My immediate object in writing this note is to suggest, with due deference, whether it might not subserve the Cause of Right and Freedom for the representatives of Massachusetts to enter their solemn and united *protest* against the virtual annihilation of the right of petition involved in the infamous resolution which has passed the House in reference to the petitions and remonstrances of *the people* upon the subject of Slavery. It seems to me that such a course is due to yourselves as well as to your constituents. Rely upon it you will in so doing meet response of approbation from any true son of Massachusetts. The common sense — the heart — the intellect of the State will be with you. The Legislature of Massachusetts will sustain you, the *people* will answer " well done " !

I have no doubt that all or mostly all of the representatives of the State would be ready to sign such a protest.

The occasion seems to me to demand it.

Excuse these suggestions from a stranger and believe me cordially and most sincerely

Thy friend

JOHN G. WHITTIER.

P. S. I shall be in Philadelphia for a week or ten days. A letter addressed to me care Benjamin S. Jones, Arch St., would reach me.

J. G. W.

AMESBURY, ESSEX Co., 12th 4th mo., 1837.

HON. JOHN Q. ADAMS:

Dear Friend, — I am requested to inform thee that at a meeting of the Board of Managers of the Massachusetts Anti-Slavery Society held in Boston on the 10th inst., Francis Jackson, Esq., in the chair, it was unanimously voted to invite thee to be present at the New England Anti-Slavery Convention to be held in Boston on the last Tuesday of May next.

We do not offer the invitation with the wish of inducing thee to take any step inconsistent with thy previously avowed sentiments. We invite thee to be a spectator of the proceedings of the friends of Liberty assembled from all parts of New England to consider subjects of the most vital importance to the whole country.

The topics which will be discussed are: 1, Texas; 2, District of Columbia; 3, Slave trade between the States; 4, Right of persons claimed as fugitive slaves to a jury trial; 5, duty of the Free States. If on any of these subjects (especially Texas) we could be favored with thy views, it would be a source of high gratification to the members of the Convention, and no doubt productive of great good to the cause of Liberty and Humanity. A line for the expression of thy determination in regard to this invitation would be received with pleasure.

Truly thy friend,
JOHN G. WHITTIER.

HON. JOHN Q. ADAMS.

NEW YORK, 3rd 1st mo., 1838.

DEAR FRIEND, — Allow me to assure thee in behalf of myself, and the friends of freedom in this city, of our grateful sense of thy services in support of the rights of the citizens and the Constitution of the United States.

The people are rousing themselves at this new aggression of the 21st ultimo. East, West, and North the land is shaking with indignant agitation; and before one month a flood of remonstrances will be rolled upon a recreant Congress. From Massachusetts, Connecticut, and New Jersey and Pennsylvania, we hear of a simultaneous movement to petition for the rescinding of this resolution. By the bye, would it not be well for

the Massachusetts delegation to draw up a statement of the manner in which their freedom of
speech and the rights of their constituents have
been denied on the floor of Congress, and publish
it in the " Intelligencer " and some of the Boston
papers? Would not all of our delegation sign
such a paper? It seems to me that something
of the kind is demanded.

Our Massachusetts Legislature will unques-
tionably speak out at this crisis, and once more
protest against these repeated violations of the
Constitution.

I need not say to thee, Go on. The thousands
who now look to thee as the champion of their
freedom of opinion, of speech and petition, will
not be disappointed.

May the God of the oppressed strengthen and
preserve thee.

Truly thy friend,
JOHN G. WHITTIER.

Whittier was of great service, too, in duties of
membership and administration connected with
his organization. One of the original members
of the American Anti-Slavery Society, he was
constant in his attendance, as far as his health
permitted, at its annual meetings and those of
the Massachusetts Anti-Slavery Society, and he
was for a while one of the vice-presidents of the

latter, and at various times one of the agents,
the managers, and the secretaries of the former.
In his relations with the societies he is on record
in their reports as proposing resolutions which
looked toward political action, and he was a
leading spirit in the movement that justly rent
asunder the organized abolitionist bodies on the
question of the establishment of a definite abolitionist party.

As an experienced journalist and pamphleteer
Whittier was even more effective. On July 23,
1836, he became again the editor of the Haverhill " Gazette," and when it was obvious that his
political attitude was not in great favor with the
subscribers, he associated with himself, on September 17, Dr. Jeremiah Spofford of George-
town, who was to have under his superintendence
" the political character and bearing of the paper," while Whittier, as the junior editor, was
to retain " the literary and miscellaneous department." To the modern reader, however, it is
plain that this sharing of the responsibilities did
not alter the abolitionist bias of the journal, and
we are not surprised in finding Whittier retiring
wholly from the management on December 17.
In the same year he administered through the
columns of the " Liberator " a telling rebuke
to pompous Governor Everett, who had in his
inaugural address endeavored to smooth his own

path by choking off discussions on slavery.[1]   In
1837 he edited John Quincy Adams's remarkable letters to his constituents with regard to
the right of petition to Congress, and some
selections from Harriet Martineau's writings
about America, under the title " Views of Slavery
and Emancipation," with an introduction showing that her anti-slavery sentiments were not the
result of prejudice : while endeavoring to represent our democratic civilization in its best light,

---

[1] W. S. Kennedy (*Whittier*, American Reformers Series,
100) seems to have been the first to point out that Wendell
Phillips, in the famous sentence in his Faneuil Hall speech,
"I thought those pictured lips would have broken into voice,
to rebuke the recreant American," was perhaps unconsciously
using Whittier's figure of two years previous : —

"George Washington was another signer of the Constitution. I know that he was a slaveholder ; and I have not forgotten the emotions which swelled my bosom, when in the
metropolis of New England, the Cradle of Liberty, a degener-
ate son of the Pilgrims [Peleg Sprague] pointed to his portrait,
which adorns the wall, with the thrice repeated exclamation,
— 'That Slaveholder ! ' I saw the only blot on the otherwise
bright and spotless character of the Father of his Country held
to open view — exposed by remorseless hands to sanction a
system of oppression and blood. It seemed to me like sacri-
lege. I looked upon those venerable and awful features, while
the echoes, once wakened in that old Hall by the voice of ancient Liberty, warm from the lips of Adams and Hancock and
the fiery heart of James Otis, gave back from wall and gallery
the exulting cry of 'Slaveholder,' half expecting to see the still
canvas darken with a frown, and the pictured lips part asunder with the words of rebuke and sorrow."

" a strict regard to truth and justice required her to speak of the hideous anomaly in our midst." In 1838, while in New York as a secretary of the American Anti-Slavery Society, he drew up, on the basis of a fugitive slave's story, " The Narrative of James Williams," a startling account of slaveholders' cruelties, which the society was compelled later to withdraw from circulation on account of the relative untrustworthiness of the witness. After the failure of a plan to establish an anti-slavery journal in Portland, Me., he took control, on March 15, 1838, of the "Pennsylvania Freeman," the official organ of the Pennsylvania Anti-Slavery Society.

His editorial work on the " Freeman " was less amateurish than in earlier years. There was a bit of cant about it, a little of the conventionality of humanitarianism; but it was resolute, straightforward writing, tolerant to his opponents both outside and inside the organization, and alive to opportunities for a telling stroke. He had less than usual to say about literature, but in commenting on a remark said to have been made by Pickens on the floor of Congress to the effect that the literature of the world is against the South, he quotes with effect Campbell's recent lines " To the United States of America on their striped and starred banner : "—

> " The white man's liberty in types
>   Stands blazon'd by your stars —
> But what 's the meaning of the stripes?
>   They mean your *Negroes'* scars!"

And it is interesting to find him for once turning aside from his more important task to call attention to Longfellow's anonymous "Psalm of Life," which had just appeared in the "Knickerbocker:" —

" It is very seldom that we find an article of poetry so full of excellent philosophy and common sense as the following. We know not who the author may be, but he or she is no common man or woman. These nine simple verses are worth more than all the dreams of Shelley, and Keats, and Wordsworth. They are alive and vigorous with the spirit of the day in which we live — the moral steam enginery of an age of action."

Whittier's political poems appeared in the Haverhill "Gazette," the "Liberator," the Boston "Courier," the "Pennsylvania Freeman," in collections of anti-slavery verse like "The North Star," "The Liberty Bell," and "Songs of the Free," and, indeed, wherever convenience and the occasion dictated. The place of publication mattered little, for they were copied far and wide, quoted by abolitionist orators, read aloud in abolitionist families, and declaimed by

abolitionist schoolboys, thus acquiring an importance wholly out of proportion to their number
or their artistic merit. As Garrison said in the
" Liberator," with reference to the " Stanzas "
beginning " Our fellow-countrymen in chains,"
" Our gifted brother Whittier has again seized
the great trumpet of Liberty, and blown a blast
that shall ring from Maine to the Rocky Mountains."

In 1837, while Whittier was in New York,
the publisher of the " Liberator," Isaac Knapp,
collected and published these verses, under the
title of " Poems Written during the Progress of
the Abolition Question in the United States,"
without, it would appear, notifying Whittier of
his intention. A little later he himself chose for
Joseph Healy, the financial agent of the Pennsylvania Anti-Slavery Society, the material for
his " Poems," which appeared in 1838. Both
volumes were tracts for the abolitionist propaganda. The first was illustrated by the familiar
woodcuts that bore the legends " Am I not a
man and a brother?" and " Am I not a woman
and a sister?" The second bore the motto from
Coleridge, " 'There is a time to keep silence,'
saith Solomon; but when I proceeded to the first
verse of the fourth chapter of the Ecclesiastes,
'and considered all the oppressions that are
done under the sun, and beheld the tears of such

as were oppressed, and they had no comforter;
and on the side of the oppressors there was
power;' I concluded this was *not* the time to
keep silence; for Truth should be spoken at all
times, but more especially at those times when
to speak Truth is dangerous." With the exception of the "Vaudois Teacher" and "Bind up
thy tresses, thou beautiful one," towards the end
of the book, the 1837 volume contained nothing
but anti-slavery matter, and the 1838 edition
printed the anti-slavery poems first, adding some
of his religious and reform pieces, and a very
few historical verses.

These early political verses, most of which are
retained in the later editions, were only of transient importance. It is with difficulty that we
can now understand the circumstances that occa-
sioned them; we must know contemporary history to appreciate their allusions. But it is not
difficult to realize that they were at that time
effective. They are not blundering verses. The
lines run smoothly, the rhythms ring. They
expostulate, they plead, they satirize; and in
every case they reach their mark. Only a deeply
reflective mind could thus search out the real
issues; only the trained hand could thus regularly
hit the target. Two or three, such as "The
Yankee Girl" and "The Slave-Ships," are in
narrative form, but the mass of his work was

purely expository, — editorials in verse. He laments his dead brothers-at-arms, he writes hymns for anniversaries, he comments on current events, taking every good opportunity for striking a strong blow for the cause, by amplifying a fine passage in an anti-slavery speech or seizing hold of some rash act or utterance on the other side. In " The Hunters of Men," he reveals, as in a cartoon, the whole force of the pious and respected Colonization Society riding at the heels of the free blacks like hunters after a fox.

> " Gay luck to our hunters! how nobly they ride
>   In the glow of their zeal, and the strength of their pride!
>   The priest with his cassock flung back on the wind,
>   Just screening the politic statesman behind;
>   The saint and the sinner, with cursing and prayer,
>   The drunk and the sober, ride merrily there.
>   And woman, kind woman, wife, widow, and maid,
>   For the good of the hunted, is lending her aid:
>   Her foot 's in the stirrup, her hand on the rein,
>   How blithely she rides to the hunting of men! "

In " Expostulation " he drives home the unanswerable inconsistency of political equality and domestic slavery : —

> " Shall every flap of England's flag
>   Proclaim that all around are free,
>   From farthest Ind to each blue crag
>   That beetles o'er the Western Sea ?
>   And shall we scoff at Europe's kings,
>   When Freedom's fire is dim with us,
>   And round our country's altar clings
>   The damning shade of Slavery's curse ? "

And in "The New Year" he lashes the subserviency of Northern politicians: —

> "Yet, shame upon them! there they sit,
>   Men of the North, subdued and still;
> Meek, pliant poltroons, only fit
>   To work a master's will.
>
> "Sold, — bargained off for Southern votes, —
>   A passive herd of Northern mules,
> Just braying through their purchased throats
>   Whate'er their owner rules."

Meanwhile he points prophetically and unerringly to the growing demand of the people of the North and West for immediate emancipation: —

> "East, West, and North, the shout is heard,
>   Of freemen rising for the right:
> Each valley hath its rallying word, —
>   Each hill its signal light.
>
> "O'er Massachusetts' rocks of gray,
>   The strengthening light of freedom shines,
> Rhode Island's Narragansett Bay,
>   And Vermont's snow-hung pines!
>
> "From Hudson's frowning palisades
>   To Alleghany's laurelled crest,
> O'er lakes and prairies, streams and glades,
>   It shines upon the West."

It was thus plain that Whittier's humanitarian aspirations overshadowed all his other interests in verse. He wrote little during the period under consideration which did not directly con-

cern reform. One long poem, indeed, "Mogg
Megone," which he began in 1830, was published
in book form in 1836, and marks the culmination of his youthful enthusiasm in New England
legend, and of his effort to retell the old tales of
the early settlers in the fashion of Scott. Whittier himself grew to dislike "Mogg Megone,"
and finally banished it from the body of his
collected poems, reprinting it in an appendix,
with the derogatory comment that it then suggested to him "a big Indian in his war-paint,
strutting about in Sir Walter Scott's plaid." But
the poem, in spite of its obvious defects, does
not deserve the obloquy it has received. I think
I may perhaps speak for many country boys in
Whittier's own district forty years later when I
say that nothing that had been written of Colonial
times seemed to us so vivid, not even Cooper's
novels. For it dealt with the New England
epos, rather than with that of the Middle or
Western States; it had something of the effect
of Parkman in the emphasis it threw on the warfare of France and England, Catholicism and
Protestantism; and the figures of the base fron-
tiersman, the great Sachem, the daring girl who
struck so boldly for revenge when she saw her
lover's scalp, the Jesuit plotting for the supre-
macy of France in America, whose great plans
she thus ruined — slight as they are, are figures

deeply typical of the great forces then at strife. Whittier failed when Scott succeeded, we must admit, though it is hard to see why. A feud of an overbearing Scottish prince with the marauding Trossack clans may well seem less noble to our minds than the romance of our own pioneers, on whose success hung the welfare of our nation; the little Scottish lakes are no more beautiful than our own. But Scott made his forays immortal, and ours are not yet fitly chronicled. Perhaps when the past takes its just place in perspective, we may have novels and romantic poems that make the life of the pioneers shine out again, and perhaps, when the proper medium has been found, we shall see that Whittier was in his youth unwittingly near the heart of the secret. Certainly we may now acknowledge that in the poem he came to despise he had stumbled for a moment on the tune of the rapid and musical narrative and descriptive verse which in later years he handled so skilfully : —

> " Ah, Mogg Megone !— what dreams are thine,
>   But those which love's own fancies dress, —
>   The sum of Indian happiness ! —
> A wigwam, where the warm sunshine
> Looks in among the groves of pine, —
> A stream, where, round thy light canoe,
> The trout and salmon dart in view,
> And the fair girl, before thee now,
> Spreading thy mat with hand of snow,
> Or plying, in the dews of morn,

Her hoe amidst thy patch of corn,
Or offering up, at eve, to thee
Thy birchen dish of hominy ! "

With so slight a poetical product closed the
critical period in Whittier's life. After a bitter
struggle he had submitted his career to the
chances of an extravagant and ill-informed
humanitarian movement, and that unselfish act
made him for the best years of his life a man of
action rather than a man of letters — a reformer,
a missionary, a politician, rather than a poet.
At thirty-five, he found himself, like Dante, in
an obscure wood, searching for the true road,
tempted and threatened by the great forces of
his time. Milton, Burke, the servants of great
causes, his own Quaker forerunners, the saints
and martyrs and crusaders of old — these and
not Virgil were the guides that showed him the
path of duty. Once found, he followed it without turning back, and it was not until he was
becoming an old man that the roads joined again
and he could devote himself entirely to letters.
Meantime the dross in his nature was to be purified by poverty, by abstinence, by isolation, by
devotion.

CHAPTER V

DURING the twenty long and painful years
which passed between the first stirrings of the
third party and the full organization of the
Black Republicans, the twenty years which
the nation needed to swing slowly into line with
the principles of the little band of political abolitionists, Whittier was almost continually a pris-
oner at Amesbury, fast bound by ill health and
poverty. In the summer of 1840 he made sundry
visits and attended the yearly meeting of the
Society of Friends at Newport. In the autumn
he twice tried to start on a little journey to
Halifax, but was not sufficiently strong. In
1841 he for a few weeks accompanied the English philanthropist, Joseph Sturge, a wealthy
fellow Quaker and abolitionist, as his guide on
part of a tour through the important cities of
the East, in the interests of the cause, but was
more than once obliged through increasing in-
disposition to return for recuperation. In 1844–
45 he lived for about six months in Lowell,

while editing the "Middlesex Standard." In
1845 he thought again of going to the West, but
found it impossible to carry out his plan. In
1845 and 1848 he visited Washington in behalf
of the abolitionists. But these somewhat stern
diversions, with his little trips in the immediate
vicinity and to Boston, were almost the only
breaks in continuous residence. His health was
always uncertain, and not unfrequently he was
severely ill. In 1847 he wrote: " I have of late
been able to write but little, and that mostly for
the papers, and I have scarcely answered a letter
for a month past. I dread to touch a pen. Whenever I do, it increases the dull wearing pain in
my head, which I am scarcely ever free from." [1]
And again in 1851: " I am slowly recovering
from the severest illness I have known for years,
the issue of which, at one time, was to me ex-
ceedingly doubtful. Indeed, I scarcely know
now how to report myself, but I am better, and
full of gratitude to God that I am permitted
once more to go abroad and enjoy this beautiful
springtime. The weather now is delightfully
warm and bright, and the soft green of the
meadows is climbing our hills. It is luxury to
live. One feels at such times terribly rooted to
this world : old Mother Earth seems sufficient
for us." [2]

[1] Pickard, *Life*, i. 319.   [2] *Ibid.* i. 355.

To this chronic weakness of health, which modern medicine with its greater insistence on hygiene could probably have greatly obviated, was added the burden of straitened means. The farm had been sold and the pleasant little house at Amesbury had been bought. There was therefore a habitation for his mother, his sister, and himself, but whence could come the funds for their simple living? Cut off from regular editorial work, from acting as a paid secretary of an anti-slavery society, and from the possible resource of lecturing, he was dependent entirely upon his pen. But occasional poems and tales and essays brought little under any circumstances; the magazines shunned, as a rule, the contributions of an abolitionist; his royalties were small; his heart, too, was almost wholly wrapped up in devotion to an apparently lost cause, and was in no mood for pure letters. Nevertheless he struggled on as best he could, sustained by the double frugality of a Quaker and a New Englander. In 1847 he accepted with pleasure a post as corresponding editor of Dr. Bailey's "National Era," published in Washington as the mouthpiece of the "new organization" or political abolitionists, properly called the American and Foreign Anti-Slavery Society, and the slender but regular salary was his mainstay throughout the remainder of this period. Even with this assistance his financial situation was a critical one, and about 1857 he escaped disaster only through the kind offices of a philanthropic abolitionist.

To the limitations of illness and poverty were added those of loneliness and disappointed ambition. With a mind that adapted itself with astonishing flexibility to new conditions, and was thus just at the beginning of its growth, he was confined to the routine of a country village. Fond of women and desirous of marriage, he was withheld not only by ill health and straitened means, but by respect for his mother's feelings, for a devout Quakeress could not have lived under the same roof with a daughter-in-law that did not share her creed. It was the wreck of all his purposes. He could no longer dream of success in journalism or in politics: he was pledged to an unpopular cause. Worse yet, he was pledged to the side of that cause where duty was less clear. Garrison's path was plain. His voice was the first to be raised for immediate, unconditional emancipation, to be secured through the moral regeneration of the American people. He was the founder of a religion whose creed was freedom to the slave. How the problem could be worked out practically was no concern of his, nor could his attention be diverted from his essential tenet. Was the Bible against it, then the Bible was wrong; did the church oppose, then the church must be reformed; did the Constitution forbid, then the Constitution must be destroyed; was union impossible under such conditions, then death to the Union. Never was extremist more logically severe. He was a man of one great moral idea, which, eventually shared by millions, brought about tremendous changes by awful means. Whittier, on the other hand, was more concerned with practical results. His first anti-slavery writing had dealt with the expediency of justice, and he continually served his cause by indicating the manner in which public opinion could be influenced and the slow legislative steps that must be taken to bring about the great event. But to attempt to lead a nation step by step toward such a tremendous reform was to enter on an unknown path in an unexplored wilderness. Mistake had to follow mistake; success was always doubtful until experience brought accurate knowledge. The way was one of compromise: as a practical reformer he had often to pass by the house of his friends and lodge with his enemies, and the goal seemed even more distant when approached by such circuitous means.

Indeed, we may wonder, though we find no indication of such a thing, whether in so practical a mind as Whittier's there could arise no doubts as to the truth of his main generalization, no tormenting suspicion that the sudden emancipation of a nation of slaves might loose economic forces impossible to control, endanger the prosperity of the free, and plunge the negro into an unsuspected gulf of pauperism and the new but scarcely less potent slavery that a commercial society imposes upon the weak. Of the real negro, his capacities and limitations, he had, like his fellows, only a dim idea, based largely on theoretic speculation, and he would have had less confidence could he at any time have foreseen the blackness of war and reconstruction and the perplexity that even now envelops us.

To dissipate the clouds of melancholy bred by Whittier's disadvantages in strength and substance and companionship, his wrecked ambitions, and his exposed position on the skirmishing line of a dangerous expedition, three forces acted powerfully,— his strenuous New England training, his quietistic religious faith, and his simple-hearted devotion to his cause.

In the character produced by the peculiar New England environment there is latent — side by side with garrulousness, inquisitiveness, and the innate desire for community building — a certain reticence, a self-centred tendency that thrives in solitude, that wishes only to be let alone. We know it best in letters through

Thoreau, who put into books the happiness his independent mind found in isolation; but all New England villages have their parallel cases of men and women whose only eccentricity lies in a desire, often reaching a morbid height, to be free from the trammels of community life. Theoretically even we could predict such a tendency, and such extreme examples of it, from a training which on all sides, political and moral, threw so strong an emphasis on the rights and functions of the individual — on the doctrine that the happiness of a being, like the weal of his soul, was of his own making. In Whittier's mind lay no morbidness, but there was naught in all he had seen and experienced to make him fear his comparative isolation or to grow weak under it.

Religiously also he was accoutred to fight his ills. As a child he seems to have submitted almost passively to his doctrinal environment, and in early manhood to have been influenced powerfully only by the magnificent Quaker tenet of the absolute equality of all persons before their Maker, revealed in many a traditional observance. In middle life the faith of the Friends grew stronger within him, and in his years of disappointment two other tenets became clearer: the quietism, the openness of the soul, nourished by frugality and abstinence, that purifies the mind ; and that greater tenet — so absurd to the dry logic of the eighteenth century, but less repugnant in the romantic period of the nineteenth, and now so consonant with our wider knowledge of the mind's extraordinary powers — that to the soul thus open comes a strange inspiration, the actual prompting of the spirit, the inner light from God.

That Whittier chafed under his spiritual limitations and restrictions, and found this light hard to seek, is apparent from a letter to his friend Richard Mott, written in November, 1840 : —

" I have to lament over protracted seasons of doubt and darkness, to shrink back from the discovery of some latent unfaithfulness and insincerity, to find evil at the bottom of seeming good, to abhor myself for selfishness and pride and vanity, which at times manifest themselves, — in short, to find the law of sin and death still binding me. My temperament, ardent, impetuous, imaginative, powerfully acted upon from without, keenly susceptible to all influences from the intellectual world, as well as to those of nature, in her varied manifestations, is, I fear, ill adapted to that quiet, submissive, introverted state of patient and passive waiting for direction and support under these trials and difficulties. I think often of our meeting at Rhode Island,

and at times something of a feeling of regret
comes over me, that I am so situated as not to
be permitted to enjoy the company and the care
and watchful ministrations of those whose labors
have been signally owned by the Great Head of
the church. Sitting down in our small meeting,
and feeling in myself and in the meeting generally a want of life, and of the renewing baptism
of that Spirit which alone can soften the hard-
ness and warm the coldness of the heart, I sigh
for the presence and the voices of the eminent
and faithful laborers in the Lord's vineyard. I
know that this out-looking of the spirit, this
craving of the eye and of the ear, is wrong, but
in the depths of spiritual weakness, is it not
natural to crave the support even of an earthly
arm?" [1]

But that his mind was deeply affected by his
religious beliefs and upheld in despondency is
plain from an incident to which he refers : —

"Did I mention to thee in my letter from
Newport a circumstance in relation to Richard
Mott? On Fifth day evening, I called to see
J. J. Gurney, agreeable to his request, in refer-
ence to abolition matters. After our interview
was over, Richard Mott followed me to the door
and wished to accompany me to my lodgings.
During our walk he told me he knew not how it

[1] Pickard, *Life*, i. 262.

was or why, but that his mind had been drawn into a deep and extraordinary exercise of sympathy with me; that he had been sensible of a deep trial and exercise in my own mind; that he had felt it so strongly that he could not rest easy without informing me of it, although he had heard nothing and seen nothing to produce this conviction in his mind. He felt desirous to offer me the language of encouragement, to urge me to put aside every weight that encumbers, and to look unto Him who was able to deliver from every trial. I confess I was startled. Firmly as I believed the Quaker doctrine on this subject, its personal application to myself in a manner so utterly inexplicable by merely human reasoning awed me. I said little to him, but enough to show him something of the state of my mind. Pray for me that I may not suffer this most evident day of the Lord's visitation to pass over and leave me as before." [1]

At all events, his heart was full of unselfish devotion to God's service in the help of man : —

"But alas, I am laying out work for others, while I am myself well-nigh powerless! What Providence has in store for me I know not, but my heart is full of thankfulness that I have been permitted to do something for the cause of humanity, and that with all my sins and errors

[1] *Ibid.* i. 261, from a letter to Ann E. Wendell.

I have not been suffered to live wholly for my-self." [1]

We now turn to the general political move-ment of the period, to the share of the abolition-ists in it, and to the part that Whittier him-self played through his personal influence and through his writings, both in prose and in verse.

Nowhere is American history more splendidly interesting than between 1840 and 1860, for there one may see the rapid development of the irrepressible conflict between two great and antagonistic economic systems, each fully ex-panded. The breach was at first the merest rift, a theoretical weakness, the moral element of danger which Garrison was the first to proclaim insistently in 1831. Jackson's strong handling of nullification seemed to presage that the Union was still so strong that nothing could shake it, and by 1840, though the number of discontented theorists in the North was growing larger, there were only the faintest signs of a party that would base itself on emancipation. But the greediness of the South for further slave territory, and the resulting annexation of Texas and war with Mexico, swelled further the ranks of discontent in the North and strengthened its determination not to endure the extension of the Southern system. That determination had its natural

[1] Pickard, *Life*, i. 338.

corollary in the increasing dislike to even the
incidental applications of the Southern system in Northern territory, — to the necessary
enforcement of fugitive slave laws that were
wholly logical and proper under a federalistic
conception of the Union.

The compromise of 1850 marked the turning
point. The last effort had been made. Both
systems had grown to the full; each had made
every allowance to the other; could they exist
side by side? The old compromisers were passing away, and in their place grew up a race
of politicians of another sort: the arrogant
Davis, insistent upon the safeguards of the
Southern system and the vested rights of the
minority; the solemn and misguided Seward,
with his law "higher" than the law; Douglas,
elfish spirit of the new Western democracy,
demolishing and unable to rebuild; and that
better spirit of the West, the slow and uncouth
Lincoln, in whose patient humanity lay the
nation's hope.

The new legislation was sudden and rash.
The repeal of the Missouri Compromise and the
promulgation of the doctrine of popular sover-
eignty threw the whole country into turmoil by
setting one man's hand against another in
Kansas. The Dred Scott decision appalled the
North and delighted the South by affirming that

a freed slave could not become a citizen. Popular feeling grew stronger in both sections. The South, exasperated at the thought of being restricted in territory and becoming a minority, refused to modify her system in such a way that the majority could properly protect it, but pushed forward her rights at every turn. The North, feeling herself in the majority, was impatient of just demands. Strife in Kansas, the burning of Lawrence, the dastardly murders of John Brown, the outrageous personalities of Sumner's speech and the more outrageous assault upon him, the inevitable friction in the enforcement of the fugitive slave laws, inflamed the minds of all citizens. The Democratic party, purged of a few Free-Soilers, became distinctly pro-slavery. The Whig party, never securely based, crumbled away. A new party arose, distinctly anti-slavery in character, taking rightfully an old name, though on another issue. Growing with great rapidity, it polled a large vote in 1856 for a bad candidate, and by 1860 it was completely organized and clearly successful. The majority was now in power, and the Republican platform, though conservative in the extreme, meant that the Northern economic system of free labor should be dominant.

The new party was preëminently one of intelligent men, who had arrived at their conclusions through thought, reading, and discussion. The presidential campaigns of 1856 and 1860 were educational campaigns, and so were many local and minor campaigns that preceded them. And in this information and education of the public the abolitionists had certainly taken the lead. The anti-slavery party was not solely the result of their ministrations. The best arguments are facts. It was the fact of an antiquated economic system entrenched in the South, and carrying numerous national evils in its train, that convinced the minds of men that this system must be destroyed or modified, or at least confined to a specially defined area, where its evils could be minimized. But in the propaganda of the indubitable fact, the abolitionists, in spite of their extreme position, their exasperating positiveness, and at times their plain fanaticism, carried the banner.

As I have already explained, the abolitionists were, by 1840, divided into two distinct parties, one under the leadership of Garrison, holding fast to the moral regeneration of the public, and the other, without a leader, believing in political agitation and organization. The Garrisonian party moved rapidly but logically to an extreme position. If slavery be the great sin of the land, but yet countenanced by the law of the country and enforced within the limits of many

states, then the righteous must hold that the law
is false and that safety lies only in breaking all
bonds of union with these states. In April,
1842, Garrison dwelt in the "Liberator" on
"the duty of making the REPEAL OF THE UNION
between the North and the South the grand
rallying-point until it be accomplished, or slavery
cease to pollute our soil. We are for throwing
all the means, energies, actions, purposes, and
appliances of the genuine friends of liberty and
republicanism into this one channel, and for
measuring the humanity, patriotism, and piety
of every man by this one standard. This question can no longer be avoided, and a right decision
of it will settle the controversy between freedom
and slavery." [1]

In May, he placed at the head of his editorial
column this declaration : "*A repeal of the union
between northern liberty and southern slavery
is essential to the abolition of the one and the
preservation of the other.*" [2]

On October 30, addressing a turbulent meeting
in Boston at the time of the Latimer case, Wendell Phillips said, in his indignation : —

"We presume to believe the Bible outweighs
the statute-book. When I look upon these
crowded thousands, and see them trample on
their consciences and the rights of their fellow-

---

[1] *William Lloyd Garrison*, iii. 52.   [2] *Ibid.* iii. 56.

men, at the bidding of a piece of parchment, I say, my CURSE be on the Constitution of these United States!"[1]

At the annual meeting of the Massachusetts Anti-Slavery Society in January, 1843, Garrison secured the passage of the following resolution :

"*Resolved*, That the compact which exists between the North and the South is 'a covenant with death and an agreement with hell' — involving both parties in atrocious criminality — and should be immediately annulled."[2]

Men holding such opinions would not vote. Their motto was "no union with slaveholders," political, religious, or personal. This disunion sentiment was soon held by a comparatively large number of abolitionists, and was officially accepted by many county and state organizations in the East and West. It led logically to the more radical doctrine that the North was justified in breaking violently away from the South, and to the aid furnished to John Brown in the Harper's Ferry *fiasco*. At the Disunion Convention of 1857 it was "*Resolved*, That the sooner the separation takes place, the more peaceful it will be; but that peace or war is *a secondary consideration*, in view of our present perils. Slavery must be conquered, 'peaceably if we can, forcibly if we must.'"[3]

[1] *Ibid*. iii. 66.　　[2] *Ibid*. iii. 88.　　[3] *Ibid*. iii. 457.

And at the Boston meeting in Tremont Temple, on the day John Brown was hanged, Garrison virtually approved his deed and his plan : —

"Whenever there is a contest between the oppressed and the oppressor, — the weapons being equal between the parties, — God knows that my heart must be with the oppressed, and always against the oppressor. Therefore, whenever commenced, I cannot but wish success to all slave insurrections. I thank God when men who believe in the right and duty of wielding carnal weapons are so far advanced that they will take those weapons out of the scale of despotism, and throw them into the scale of freedom. It is an indication of progress, and a positive moral growth; it is one way to get up to the sublime platform of non-resistance; and it is God's method of dealing retribution upon the head of the tyrant. Rather than see men wearing their chains in a cowardly and servile spirit, I would, as an advocate of peace, much rather see them breaking the head of the tyrant with their chains. Give me, as a non-resistant, Bunker Hill, and Lexington, and Concord, rather than the cowardice and servility of a Southern slave-plantation." [1]

With such disunion sentiments — treasonable as we may think them now — Whittier was at

---

[1] *William Lloyd Garrison*, iii. 492.

times partly in sympathy. In March, 1842, he wrote to his abolitionist friend Sewall: " I fear we shall get dragged into a war after all,— a war in defence of the vilest negro traffic existing anywhere save on the African coast! It is un- endurable! And if Texas is to be added to us, as there are no doubtful indications, let us say, Disunion before Texas!" [1] And a stanza of his "Texas" (1844) was first published as

> " Make our Union-band a chain,
> We will snap its links in twain,
> We will stand erect again!"

In all but rare moments, however, he was consistently on the side of progress according to law, a firm believer in securing political results through political as well as moral agitation. The enormous popular force required to secure disunion would be more than enough, he was accustomed to declare, to secure union with emancipation. The work of his life lay in the building up of an anti-slavery party such as he described in 1841–42 in writing to the English humanitarian and philanthropist, his friend Joseph Sturge : —

" The two great political parties in the United States, radically disagreeing in almost all other points, are of one heart and mind in opposing emancipation ; not, I suppose, from any real

[1] Pickard, *Life*, i. 288.

affinity to, or love for the 'peculiar institution,' but for the purpose of securing the votes of the slaveholders, who, more consistent than the Northern abolitionists, refuse to support any man for office who is not willing to do homage to slavery. The competition between these two parties for Southern favor is one of the most painful and disgusting spectacles which presents itself to the view of a stranger in the United States. To every well-wisher of America it must be a matter of interest and satisfaction to know that there is a growing determination in the free States to meet the combination of slaveholders in behalf of slavery by one of freemen in behalf of liberty; and thus compel the party politicians, on the ground of expediency, if not of principle, to break from the thraldom of the slave power, and array themselves on the side of freedom." [1]

The same doctrine is laid down in his address to the citizens of Amesbury and Salisbury, after the assault on Sumner : —

"Fearing I may not be able to attend the meeting this evening, I beg leave to say a word to my fellow-citizens. I need not say how fully I sympathize with the object of the meeting, nor speak of my grief for the sufferings and danger of a beloved friend, now nearer and dearer than

[1] Joseph Sturge, *A Visit to the United States in 1841*, 230.

ever, stricken down at his post of duty, for his manly defence of freedom; nor of my mingled pity, horror, and indignation in view of the atrocities in Kansas. It seems to me to be no time for the indulgence of mere emotions. Neither railing nor threats befit the occasion. It is our first duty to inquire why it is that the bad men in power have been emboldened to commit the outrages of which we complain. Why is it that the South has dared to make such experiments upon us? The North is not united for freedom, as the South is for slavery. We are split into factions, we get up paltry side issues, and quarrel with and abuse each other, and the Slave Power, as a matter of course, takes advantage of our folly. That evil power is only strong through our dissensions. It could do nothing against a united North. The one indispensable thing for us is Union. Can we not have it? Can we not set an example in this very neighborhood, — Whigs, Democrats, Free-Soilers, and Americans, joining hands in defence of our common liberties? We must forget, *forgive*, and UNITE. I feel a solemn impression that the present opportunity is the last that will be offered us for the peaceful and constitutional remedy of the evil which afflicts us. The crisis in our destiny has come: the hour is striking of our final and irrevocable choice. God grant that it may be rightfully made.   Let us not be betrayed into threats.   Leave violence where it belongs, with the wrong-doer.   It is worse than folly to talk of fighting Slavery, when we have not yet agreed to vote against it.   Our business is with poll-boxes, not cartridge-boxes; with ballots, not bullets.   The path of duty is plain : God's providence calls us to walk in it.   Let me close by repeating, Forget, *forgive*, and UNITE." [1]

With these aims in view he labored faithfully for the Liberty party and the Free-Soil party, and later for the Republican party, not pushing his companions further or faster than they would go, and willing to join with them in platforms that said nothing about abolition, provided he was sure that they were really antagonistic to the dangerous economic system to which the South was wedded.   From talk of armed interference he kept aloof, and his letter to Sumner, after John Brown's raid, shows how, unlike Emerson, Thoreau, Higginson, and Garrison, he was firm in his opposition to the use of unlawful means, as well as shrewd in seeing how the disaster could best be turned to political account : —

"I have expressed my views of the Harper's Ferry outbreak.   I am anxious that our Republican members of Congress should meet the matter fairly, and unequivocally condemn *all*

[1] Pickard, *Life*, i. 382.

filibustering, whether for freedom or slavery.
I like Trumbull's motion — Harper's Ferry is
the natural result of the slaveholders' forays
into Kansas, and both should be considered
together. The distinction should be made clear
between the natural sympathy with the man and
approval of his mad, and, as I think, most dangerous and unjustifiable act. The North is sound
on this point — there are few who approve of the
raid over the border." [1]

The foregoing summary of the political movement of the period and of the progress of abolitionism is necessary for a clear understanding of
Whittier's acts and opinions; for we must not
forget that he was still a reformer and not yet a
man of letters. We may now pass to his own
share in the propaganda.

We have already called attention to the pro-
found differences of opinion among the abolitionists as to the methods and means to be
employed in reaching their end. The first *crux*
was the part which women should play in the
movement, a point involved in the famous Clerical Appeal of 1837. Though Whittier censured
the Appeal, and though he believed himself in
the participation of women, he thought that
prudence demanded that the abolitionists refrain
from awakening against themselves any strong

[1] Pickard, *Life*, ii. 425.

popular prejudice. His letter of August 14, 1837, to the Misses Grimké, who had not only spoken with great effect in public, but were being urged to publish a set of letters on the subject of women's rights, shows precisely his point of view : —

"I am anxious, too, to hold a long conversation with you on the subject of war, human government, and church and family government. The more I reflect on this subject, the more difficulty I find, and the more decidedly I am of opinion that we ought to hold all these matters far aloof from the cause of abolition. Our good friend H. C. Wright, with the best intentions in the world, is doing great injury by a different course. He is making the anti-slavery party responsible in great degree for his, to say the least, startling opinions. I do not censure him for them, although I cannot subscribe to them in all their length and breadth. But let him keep them distinct from the cause of emancipation. [He instances also Garrison's policy in inserting in the 'Liberator' articles on Grahamism and no-governmentism as an injustice to the subscribers to the cause, who desire to have their money spent for the spread of the doctrine of immediate emancipation.]

"In regard to another subject, 'the rights of woman,' you are now doing much and nobly to vindicate and assert the rights of woman. Your lectures to crowded and promiscuous audiences on a subject manifestly in many of its aspects *political*, interwoven with the framework of the government, are practical and powerful assertions of the right and duty of woman to labor side by side with her brother for the welfare and redemption of the world. Why, then, let me ask, is it necessary for you to enter the lists as controversial writers on this question? Does it not *look*, dear sisters, like abandoning in some degree the cause of the poor and miserable slave, sighing from the cotton plantation of the Mississippi, and whose cries and groans are forever sounding in our ears, for the purpose of arguing and disputing about some trifling oppression, political or social, which we may ourselves suffer?" [1]

Though Whittier's attitude throughout the controversy that ensued in the various anti-slavery societies was sensible and discreet, the feelings of Garrison and the Boston abolitionists were plainly hurt, and they grew more and more to regard him as a backslider. And when the second *crux* appeared, the question whether the "Liberator" was the official organ of abolitionism and should devote itself more exclusively to that special cause, and when Whittier was again

[1] C. H. Birney, *The Grimké Sisters*, 203.

found siding with the New York group of political workers on the basis of expediency, the breach became complete. Garrison, in his blunt way, declared that Whittier's withdrawal from the "Pennsylvania Freeman" on account of ill health was no great loss,[1] and in the "Liberator" for August 12, 1842, he spoke thus harshly of his old friend : —

"Let us now trace this affair a little further. Let us see what has become of those who once stood so prominently before the American people as abolitionists of the most flaming character, and who separated from the old organization in order to show their superior zeal in the cause of emancipation by advocating it as 'men of one idea.'

"1. Where is James G. Birney? In Western 'retiracy,' waiting to be elected President of the United States, that he may have an opportunity to do something for the abolition of slavery. . . .

"6. Where is John G. Whittier? At home, we believe, but incapable of doing anything important for the cause — except to write political,

---

[1] "J. G. Whittier has retired from the editorial chair of the 'Freeman.' The time has been when we should have deeply regretted to make this announcement; but, in his present state of mind, as it respects political action and 'new organization,' and in view of the course he has thought proper to pursue in regard to the state of things in this his native commonwealth, we are reconciled to his withdrawal."

electioneering addresses for the 'Liberty party.' New organization has affected his spirit to a withering extent, and politics will complete the ruin, if he 'tarry in all the plain.'"

Garrison's chief supporters shared his feelings. Mrs. Chapman is reported to have been doubtful whether Whittier was more knave or fool, and placed him on the "clerical platform of hatred to Mr. Garrison." [1] In 1839 or 1840 Lydia Maria Child wrote as follows to Abby Hopper Gibbons : —

"In those days, I little dreamed of the painful and mortifying divisions that have since distracted our ranks. Yet a glance backward at all other reforms might have prepared me for it. The Apostles soon had those among them who came 'to spy out their liberty;' and why should I marvel at John G. Whittier, when I recollect that Barnabas himself was 'led away by their dissimulations'?

"Yet I am surprised that Whittier does not perceive the glaring fact that the Massachusetts Society is composed of men who walk abroad at noonday — who, at least, have nothing to conceal, and no necessity for assuming, while the New Organization are resorting to all manner of management and trickery, taking ground on

[1] Maria Weston Chapman, *Right and Wrong in Massachusetts* (1840), 99.

false issues, shifting ground, when that on which they stand is too obviously hollow. . . . This pretending one thing and meaning another I have no patience with." [1]

In 1840, N. P. Rogers, in the "Anti-Slavery Standard," thus proclaims him as an outsider : —

"Who could have thought, while contemplating the lofty effusions of our anti-slavery bard, that 'new organization' would ever be able to 'tame' or to 'catch' his ethereal spirit, or fetter his free limbs in its narrow harness? Alas! has it not caught him, and reduced him, and tamed him, as to all further coöperation in the enterprise of which he has ever been the ornament and pride? It may be to humble us in the dust, that star after star in our enterprise is thus starting from its sphere in the anti-slavery firmament, and disappearing like an exploded meteor. Whittier at length goes out, we fear, among the other wandering luminaries. We speak it with grief, for we have gloried in his light and beauty. But, henceforth, we look for him no longer blazing in the anti-slavery van, bearing his shield gallantly abreast of the 'Liberator,' — celebrating the triumphs of freedom in deathless verse, and bursting forth on tyranny in volcanic explosion, as it developed itself from time to time, under the Ithuriel touches of our

[1] S. H. Emerson, *Life of Abby Hopper Gibbons* (1883), 146.

movement. We look no longer for his banner in the anti-slavery field. He is transferred to another service." [1]

And even as late as 1848 Sidney Howard Gay, the editor of the "National Anti-Slavery Standard," deemed it necessary to prefix the following words to Lowell's review of Whittier's poems (Dec. 21, 1848) : —

"It is pleasant [2] to hear the completeness and beauty of the tribute of praise rendered by poet to poet; to test the *harmony* by a touch of the key-note, which, however gentle, will strike harshly upon the unpractised ear: but older abolitionists cannot forget what Mr. Lowell cannot be aware of, that in the struggle of 1840, which was a struggle for life or death to the anti-slavery cause, Whittier, the Quaker, was found side by side with the men who would have sacrificed that cause, to crush, according even to their own acknowledgment, the right of woman to plead publicly in behalf of the slave, and to cripple the influence and power of men accused of no other crime than that of holding to the old Quaker doctrine — not to go farther back — of ' resist not evil ! ' We can

[1] Quoted in W. S. Kennedy, *Whittier*, American Reformers Series, 160.

[2] The text reads, "It is *not* pleasant ; " but the *not* is obviously contrary to the sense. The author may, perhaps, have written " Is it not."

join in any praises of the genius of the poet, but
not of the man who has not the manliness and
courage to honor in his life the truths he loves
to celebrate in song."

Thus estranged, through no fault save zeal on
either side, from the body of New England abolitionists, Whittier labored long, faithfully, and
with good results in the political field of his own
district. With his little band of third party
voters he held the balance of power, and, as we
have already recounted, kept Cushing in Congress to represent the North Essex District only
because Cushing was pledged to support, in certain ways, his cause; and on one occasion, as a
candidate himself, he prevented for more than
a year the election of either of two equally un-
satisfactory candidates. Similarly it is said to
have been partly his influence that sent Rantoul
to represent the South District.

How strong his hold was on Cushing is apparent from the following diplomatic epistle from
him, apparently written in the early part of this
period: [1] —

JOHN G. WHITTIER, ESQR.

MY DEAR SIR: — Your letter dated the 3rd
inst. and postmarked the 5th, did not reach me

[1] From the original in the possession of the Misses Johnson
and Mrs. Woodman.

until this afternoon on my return from Salem, where I have been attending the Supreme Court. I write a line of reply, in great haste, for the possibility of some private conveyance to Haverhill.

I profess that I think the situation of the District of Columbia, in respect of slavery and the slave traffic, is wholly indefensible ; that I should heartily rejoice in any change for the better ; and that I should, of course, wherever I may be, favor any feasible project for attaining so desirable an end. In so representing my opinion, therefore, you have but done me justice. At the same time, however, I should be unwilling to enter Congress *pledged* to INSTITUTE *a legislative* measure, either upon this or any subject of national policy and legislation, unless it were a point directly and publicly put in issue by my own constituents ; in which case I should feel bound either to obey their instructions, or to yield my place to some other Representative.

I write you this frankly, because between you and me there should be no reservation of views on my part. But I have not time to weigh my language sufficiently for publication ; and therefore commit these few lines, uncopied, to your friendly discretion. It has repeatedly occurred to me that a judicious and temperate correspondence between you and me upon this class of topics written for the press, might be made interesting and useful in so modifying the views of the respective friends of either side of the question, as to produce a reasonable degree of harmony upon it among all New Englanders. But this is a grave enterprise, and requires consideration; and is not a thing to be thrust into the bowels of a contested election at the present moment.

As for the balloting of Monday, while I hope for the best, and am assured that good feelings obtain throughout the District, yet I am ready for any result, and cannot be disappointed.

[Signature cut out.]

NEWBURY PORT, SATURDAY AFTERNOON.

In practical politics results are effected only at the expense of much time, energy, and adroitness, and it is pleasant to find Whittier so indefatigable in his self-imposed duties. A letter of George Bradburn's to his wife, written in 1846, shows how others viewed his efforts : —

"John is one of the greatest workers, politically even, in all our State. I sometimes wonder how so fine a mind can stoop to such drudgery. But Whittier has as much benevolence as he has ideality. He knows the drudgery must be done, and, since no one else does it, will do it himself. May Heaven bless him." [1]

[1] *A Memorial of George Bradburn* (1883), 146.

An extract from a letter written by Whittier to his sister in 1845 will indicate even more plainly the way in which he patrolled his district : —

" Mother is at Haverhill. On Sixth day I carried her up, and then proceeded upon my mission among the abolitionists. Got to Haverhill, called on several of the ' Liberty men,' and finally held a meeting — a sort of impromptu affair — at which eloquent speeches were made by several gentlemen, Mr. Algernon Sydney Nichols among the rest. When it came to my turn I began with as much vehemence as Mr. Pickwick, but broke down about midway, and gradually subsided into a sort of melancholy monotone, which under other circumstances would have been very affecting. As it was, I am not very sanguine of its effect upon my audience, but, like Paul's unknown tongues, it at least edified myself. . . . From Haverhill I went to Bradford, called on Father P., heard his testimony against the come-outers ; called on the come-outers and heard theirs against Father P.,— listening with patient but non-committal civility to both,— urging all parties to forego their contentions and emulate each other in the good cause of Liberty. Then I drove down to Griffin's ; took dinner, and then he and I started for Newbury and Newburyport, where I trust we did good service." [1]

[1] Pickard, *Life*, i. 309.

But this earnest work in local politics did not preclude his personal participation in the larger field. His eye was fixed on the national issue, and he was not diverted by local issues, by temporary successes or defeats. He realized the value of every move in the great game. He helped wherever he could, most of all by his counsel. He was Joseph Sturge's guide in his effort to throw the weight of Quaker organization on the anti-slavery side; he devised petitions to the Massachusetts legislature and to Congress, and was, with Henry Wilson, delegated in 1845 to carry to Washington the Liberty petition, containing sixty thousand names, against the annexation of Texas; he urged on John P. Hale in New Hampshire politics; he aided in various coalitions, notably that by which Boutwell became governor of Massachusetts and Charles Sumner went to the Senate. In the latter case Sumner was apparently the man of Whittier's own choosing and Whittier the intermediary who persuaded Sumner to enter the scheme, and his memory of their interview at Swampscott found its place in his verse : —

" Thou knowest my heart, dear friend, and well canst guess
  That, even though silent, I have not the less
  Rejoiced to see thy actual life agree
  With the large future which I shaped for thee,
  When, years ago, beside the summer sea,
  White in the moon, we saw the long waves fall

Baffled and broken from the rocky wall,
That, to the menace of the brawling flood,
Opposed alone its massive quietude,
Calm as a fate ; with not a leaf nor vine
Nor birch-spray trembling in the still moonshine,
Crowning it like God's peace." [1]

He was alert to discover men of sincerity of
purpose and good repute with the public at
large who could represent the third party in
Congress or elsewhere. He urged John Pierpont
and Longfellow to run for Congress, and suggested many excellent nominations, as would
be expected of one who, as editor and poet,
knew the real feelings of New Englanders perhaps better than any other living man. And
when he found the moral enthusiast and the
politician combined, he was active in guiding
him by sound advice and stimulating him to
renewed effort. Sumner came to Amesbury to
consult him and was in frequent correspondence
with him,— a correspondence that had less in it
of personal friendship than of common devotion
to a great mission. The following letter of
1848, for example, is typical of many : —

" In the mean time, what will the New York
Barnburners do? Is there no hope of uniting
with them, and erecting on the ruins of the old
parties the great party of Christian Democracy
and Progress? Why try to hold on to these old

[1] *To Charles Sumner* (1854).

parties, even in name? . . . It strikes me that
it would be best not to make a nomination at
Worcester, but to appoint delegates to a general
convention of the friends of Freedom and Free
Soil, without distinction of party, the time and
place of which not to be fixed before consultation
with friends of the movement in other States.
Don't stultify yourselves by boasting of your
Whiggery. That did when Taylor was nominated. Judge Allen is right: the Whig party
is dissolved. Let your emancipated friends now
rise to the sublime altitude of men who labor for
the race, for humanity. Send out from your
convention, if you will, a long and careful statement of the facts in the case, but with it also an
appeal to the people which shall reach and waken
into vigorous life all that remains of weakness
in the North. Kindle up the latent enthusiasm
of the Yankee character, call out the grim fanaticism of the Puritan. Dare! *dare!* DARE!
as Danton told the French; that is the secret of
successful revolt. Oh, for a man! There is
the difficulty, after all. Who is to head the
movement? Hale has many of the martial qualities of a leader. As a stump orator he is second
only to John Van Buren, who, by the bye, I
would far rather see in nomination for the presidency than his father or Judge McLean. It
would be folly and suicide to nominate a shrink-

ing conservative, whose heart is not with you, and whom you must drag up to your level by main force. . . . You must have a new and bold man, one to whom old notions and practices on the question of slavery are like threads of tow, breaking with the first movement of his limbs. But this advice, however well meant on my part, is doubtless not needed. You have strong and noble men, — Adams, Howe, Phillips, Wilson, Hoar, Allen, and others. I only wish you had the power of the French provisional government; I could answer for the wisdom of your decrees." [1]

All this, it must be remembered, was in a period of turmoil and disaster, of scheming and compromising, a period that appeared inexpressibly ignoble to the simple-minded theorists who held for the pure ideal. In the world-old conflict for justice, they have the better part who, like Garrison, can stand alone, insisting on the moral regeneration of the public, and waiting for the millennium. Whittier, like all reforming politicians, chose the less ideal but equally necessary task of helping by main force to bring about the right, little by little, point by point, fighting in the ruck of it all, and open always to the charge of merely temporizing. Nor, in his special case, could he even hope to secure a politician's reward

[1] Pickard, *Life*, i. 331.

of fame. He was only doing what many others did — the plain political duty of the citizen reformer.

But Whittier's best service to the cause to which he has devoted his life was through his pen, in both his old qualities, so oddly diverse, of journalist and of poet.

In the winter of 1841–42 he took charge for a short period of the Boston "Emancipator" to relieve his old friend Joshua Leavitt, and in the autumn of 1841 he had lent similar aid to the "American and Foreign Anti-Slavery Reporter," which had been begun in New York in June, 1840, as the mouthpiece of the "new organization," the American and Foreign Anti-Slavery Society. Those were the days when Garrison was under criticism for upholding other heresies than emancipation in the "Liberator," and it was plainly this that Whittier had in mind when in April, 1841, he wrote to the "Reporter" a letter of warm commendation: "Its crowning glory is that it is precisely what it pretends to be — an *anti-slavery* paper. It adheres to its one object with singleness of purpose. It neither assails nor encourages other schemes for reform which may be abroad in society." In spite of this, the "Reporter" was a very dull sheet indeed, a mere official bulletin, not worthy of comparison with the "Liberator." The officers of the new society apparently felt this, for in the issue of September 1, 1841, the executive committee were happy " to announce that they have secured the services of John G. Whittier in the Editorial Department of the ' Reporter,' as far as the state of his health will admit." A paragraph from Whittier follows to state that " he has engaged to contribute to the Editorial Department of the ' Reporter,' as far as the state of his health and his present necessary absence from the place of publication will permit. He can promise little save an honest effort to aid the cause to which the best portion of his life has been hitherto devoted. Situated as he is, it is due to all parties concerned to say that he can be held responsible for nothing more than such articles as may bear his signature."

The same number contains articles by Whittier on Joseph Sturge and on Slavery in the District of Columbia. In the following number, that of October 1, 1841, the editor falls sturdily upon Edward Everett, whom he had so soundly berated in 1836. Everett had since then distinctly avowed an entire change of opinion on the subject of emancipation, and professed a thorough conversion to the doctrines of the abolitionists. But his nomination as minister to England had just been confirmed by the Senate, and Whittier suspected him of having intimated to interested parties that his conversion had been merely temporary : —

"Governor Everett is now in Europe. We will do him the justice to believe that the pitiful disclaimers of his political friends, in and out of Congress, have been made without his consent or even knowledge, and that in his letters to Quincy, Borden, and Jackson, he really *meant what he said.* It must, we conceive, somewhat abate his satisfaction in view of his appointment, to learn that it was only obtained by strenuous efforts on the part of his professed friends, to show that his anti-slavery professions were purely hypocritical, and that he had been mean and wicked enough to obtain abolition votes in Massachusetts *under false pretences.*"

But the executive committee must have seen the hopelessness of their effort, even with Whittier's aid. No other number of the "Reporter" appeared until June, 1842, and then there were no articles signed by Whittier and apparently none written by him.[1]

In 1844 Whittier again assumed charge of one of the many local abolitionist organs, this time the weekly "Middlesex Standard," of Lowell, the first number of which was published

[1] For the opportunity to examine the file of this now very rare periodical I am indebted to the kindness of the Library of Cornell University.

under his editorship on July 25. He took lodgings at the Temperance Hotel in Lowell, and
continued to furnish the greater part of the
original matter for the paper until October,
when Mr. C. L. Knapp, of Vermont, joined him
as an assistant. Beginning with October 31,
Whittier and Knapp were joint-editors, but the
paper was gradually turned over to the latter.
After the issue of March 13, 1845, it was consoli-
dated with the Worcester County Liberty paper,
and, as the "Worcester and Middlesex Gazette," was published both in Worcester and in
Lowell.

In the columns of this obscure sheet, only one
file of which is known to be preserved,[1] is to be
found what seems to me Whittier's best work as
a journalist. It was a new paper; he was in
complete control; he was at the height of his
power and experience; he was addressing the
men of his own county in the midst of an exciting campaign; and he was perhaps stimulated to
do his best by the strikingly vigorous life of the
young manufacturing city. Certainly he never
wrote with more freedom and energy, with less
personal reticence. In the issue of September
12, 1844, he thus welcomed Ralph Waldo Emerson's "Address Delivered in the Court House
of Concord on the 1st of August, 1844:" —

[1] In the collection of the Lowell Historical Society.

" With a glow of heart, with silently invoked blessings, we have read the address whose title is at the head of this article. We had previously, we confess, felt half indignant that, while we were struggling against the popular current, mobbed, hunted, denounced from the legislative forum, cursed from the pulpit, sneered at by wealth and fashion and shallow aristocracy, such a man as Ralph Waldo Emerson should be brooding over his pleasant philosophies, writing his quaint and beautiful essays, in his retirement on the banks of the Concord, unconcerned and 'calm as a summer morning.' . . . How *could* he sit there, thus silent? Did no ripple of the world's agitation break the quiet of old Concord? Garrison's fierce trumpet blast — Lovejoy's heroic death — the women of Boston beset by aristocratic mobs — Birney's shattered printing-presses sinking in the Ohio — that sublime old man of Quincy contending single-handed with the Slave-Power in Congress — Channing's prophet-utterances among Berkshire mountains — Pierpont's Tyrtæan words, — not even these seemed to startle the philosophic dreamer, or disturb the organ-flow of his beautiful abstractions."

An even more striking editorial was that in which, at the end of the Polk-Clay-Birney campaign, he defended himself against the charge of inconsistency in deserting Clay, his youthful verses in whose praise his opponents had not hesitated to circulate : —

" So far as we were personally concerned, we had no disposition to exaggerate the faults of the Whig candidate. His brilliant talents, his early republicanism, his splendid eloquence, excited our boyish enthusiasm and admiration. We would not rob him of one tittle of his just fame as a statesman and man of genius. But when his friends urged him upon us for the highest place in the gift of a free people, we felt bound to speak the whole truth of his present position and past history in relation to the cause of Freedom. We had no other alternative. In linking, deliberately and before the world, his destiny with the tottering cause of slavery — in closing his eyes to the signs of the times, and his ears to the shouts of the emancipated millions and the clang of breaking fetters sounding across the waters from half the nations of Europe, and placing his strong shoulders against the falling Ark of the American Baal, making himself the champion of the vilest oppression on which the sun looks,— he imposed upon the friends of the slave the stern duty of denouncing him as unfit to be the recipient of public favor; and of declaring that the man who — in the land of the Declaration of Independence, in this

Nineteenth Century, with the light of the gospel
and the free principles of the Revolution blazing around him, with the voice of the Almighty
speaking in the great events of the age and
proclaiming that the power of human despotism
is to pass away forever, and that a new era of
light, liberty, and Christian love is about to
dawn upon the world,— with the successful experiments of emancipation in the West Indies
before him — has deliberately and unreservedly
taken his stand on the side of SLAVERY, overcome the scruples of his younger and better
days, crucified his humanity, and renounced his
allegiance to republicanism and Christianity,—
is unworthy of the suffrages of a people pro-
fessedly governed by the principles of Him who
came to preach deliverance to the captive, and
the opening of the prison to them that are
bound. This duty, which he himself imposed
on us, we have fearlessly and faithfully per-
formed — in common with many others of his
early admirers and friends — men who have
watched, with a Chaldean's love, the star of his
greatness, while it rose apparently to a glorious
culmination. Lustreless and waning in its
unblessed conjunction with the malignant influences of slavery, we have been compelled to
turn from it ourselves, and warn others to do
likewise."

Similarly, he took charge, in 1845, of the Amesbury " Village Transcript," which changed its name to the " Essex Transcript " and became the organ of the third party in that district. No file of it can now be found, but Mr. Stephen Lamson, a compositor, has left the following interesting reminiscences of Whittier's relations to the paper at that period : —

" He did not pretend, or wish it understood, that he was editor of the paper ; but he was its godfather, and undertook to see that it went the way it should go. He did not sign his editorials. Often sickness or absence would prevent his coming into the office for some time, and Mr. Abner L. Bagley and Rev. Mr. Strickland would take his place. This continued about four years, when the proprietor, Mr. J. M. Pettengill, sold out, and the paper became the village organ again. . . . Mr. Whittier was then a man of thirty-seven, tall, straight, and spare, with sharp, good features, handsome face, black eyes, with a long-shaped head, and a towering intellectual forehead. He wore a Quaker medium hat, as well as coat, and used his ' thees ' and ' thous ' in conversation. He was not a fluent talker, never put on superior airs, but assumed the commonplace in his intercourse with neighbors, friends, and the villagers generally. I remember one or two stores, kept by good friends of his,— one a

Baptist deacon, the other a Friend,— where he
used to visit when going to the post office; and
it was his wont to sit on boxes and barrels, as
we have seen them crowd together in a small
village grocery store, and do his visiting, and
learn the news of the day, or talk over political
matters, — for in these two friends he found
congenial spirits. This was one of his ways of
taking recreation. In my three years' acquaintance with him, and observation of him in his
daily visits to our office to read the papers, I
noticed that if something of great importance
attracted his attention, he would nervously grasp
a pen, and thoughts that scintillated from his
brain would rush across the paper before him at
a rapid rate, in a clear, smooth, running hand
that would surprise me. When the written
pages went into the copy drawer, it would be
found in a beautiful flowing hand, with seldom
an emendation or any interlining, he held his
ideas in such perfect form and control. I used
to call it a 'lightning hand,' so rapidly did the
pen fly over the paper. His sister used to have
a literary circle to improve her young friends in
various ways. My father's adopted daughter
was a member of it, and was delighted to think
she was worthy to belong to Miss Whittier's
circle. Mr. Whittier used to lend sanction and
help to these friends of his sister, and became

acquainted with each one. He used always, when I saw him, to have something to say about this sister and about my father, and I was grateful for it."

Whittier's anonymous prose in these little anti-slavery journals may be compared with the yeoman work he did in district politics. It was transient and local in its aim and in its effects, but it was sane, shrewd, vigorous, noble writing, and Whittier would not have been himself had he not done it. His message to the people of the North at large, on the other hand, was given not in prose but in verse.

The political poems of this period are not many. Perhaps fifty, printed wherever the occasion demanded, have been preserved in later editions of his works, and there seems to be scarcely a dozen that were not republished. But though their bulk was slight, their importance was great. He was not *a* poet of his party but *the* poet. He knew the hearts of the people so well, his thought and his emotions were so representative of all the country-living Northerners, of all those whose ideas of national economics were not blinded by commerce or convention, that an increasing multitude found in him their spokesman. The mass of these poems now seem obscure or trivial. He lamented reformers who had died in their harness; he satirized his opponents; he commented freely on whatever current events needed the rapid and incisive treatment that his verse could give. All these, it would appear, must ultimately perish or be read for their antiquarian interest alone, even such superb verses as those sung by the army of Kansas emigrants: —

> " We cross the prairie as of old
>   The Pilgrims crossed the sea,
> To make the West as they the East,
>   The homestead of the free!"

Only two still ring out now after more than half a century as resonantly as they sounded then,— " Ichabod " and " Massachusetts to Virginia."

Of " Ichabod " it would be improper to speak without quoting what Whittier himself said as to its origin: —

" This poem was the outcome of the surprise and grief and forecast of evil consequences which I felt on reading the seventh of March speech of Daniel Webster in support of the ' compromise ' and the Fugitive Slave Law. No partisan or personal enmity dictated it. On the contrary, my admiration of the splendid personality and intellectual power of the great Senator was never stronger than when I laid down his speech, and, in one of the saddest moments of my life, penned my protest. I saw, as I wrote, with painful clearness, its sure results, — the Slave Power

arrogant and defiant, strengthened and encouraged to carry out its scheme for the extension
of its baleful system, or the dissolution of the
Union, the guaranties of personal liberty in the
free States broken down, and the whole country
made the hunting-ground of slave-catchers. In
the horror of such a vision, so soon fearfully fulfilled, if one spoke at all, he could only speak in
tones of stern and sorrowful rebuke.

" But death softens all resentments, and the
consciousness of a common inheritance of frailty
and weakness modifies the severity of judgment.
Years after, in ' The Lost Occasion,' I gave utterance to an almost universal regret that the
great statesman did not live to see the flag which
he loved trampled under the feet of Slavery, and,
in view of this desecration, make his last days
glorious in defence of ' Liberty and Union, one
and inseparable.' " [1]

Those whom Whittier knew best in later life
relate that he came eventually to feel that Webster was perhaps right and he wrong; that
compromise meant weary years of waiting, but
that the further and consistent pursuit of such

[1] Prefatory note in the Cambridge Edition. The title may
have been suggested by Lowell's sentence in the *National
Anti-Slavery Standard*, July 2, 1846 : " Shall not the Recording Angel write *Ichabod* after the name of this man in the
great book of Doom ? "

a policy might have successfully avoided the evils of war and of reconstruction. However that may be, the verses are, in their awful scorn, the most powerful that he ever wrote. Right or wrong, he spoke for a great part of the North and West, nay, for the world. For the poem, in much the same fashion as Browning's "Lost Leader," is becoming disassociated with any special name, and may thus remain a most remarkable expression — the most terrible in our literature — of the aversion which any mass of people may feel, especially in a democracy, for the once-worshipped leader whose acts and words, in matters of the greatest public weal, seem to retrograde.

"Massachusetts to Virginia" is, in a corresponding fashion, the one most likely to survive of a group of half a dozen poems, written in the forties, in connection with the fugitive slave cases or the annexation of Texas. They are in essence battle-songs, rallying-cries for the rousing of the people. Like "Ichabod," "Massachusetts to Virginia" is a perfect expression of sectional feeling; the summing up, in impassioned verse, of one side of a great controversy; the complete brief for the North; the rhetorically logical statement of a feeling that itself went counter to logic and to law. If the law was to be obeyed, if the constitutional contract

was not to be set aside, then property — even
were it property in men — must be respected in
one State as in another. But in the North abolitionists and compromisers alike had formulated
a higher law and were determined to ignore all
obligations based on slavery : —

> " All that a sister State should do, all that a free State may,
> Heart, hand, and purse we proffer, as in our early day ;
> But that one dark loathsome burden ye must stagger with
> alone,
> And reap the bitter harvest which ye yourselves have sown ! "

Even now it would be impossible for the
Southerner to find beauty in a presentation of
the subject so extravagant in its details, so bitter in its opposition ; but may not the poem survive, both for the swinging force of its lines and
as a brilliant example of sectional indignation,
when the occasion that prompted it is forgotten ?

To Whittier, Massachusetts and Virginia were
not names or abstractions or personifications.
His firm connection with life, his preoccupation
with people and places, forced him to visualize
where others would have generalized. The men
of Virginia *were* indignantly threatening. The
men of Massachusetts *were* indignantly defiant.
He saw both groups as individuals and made
one shout to the other. His poem was no aca-
demic figure of speech ; it was, as it were, a com-

posite photograph of actuality, and may, therefore, live as a type of all cases in which one sister community resolutely defies another.

The final charm lies in the details of Whittier's visualization of Massachusetts. He was never fond of pure literature. The books he cared most for were books of travel. He loved people and towns, he thought of the world as a great picture, and of New England and especially of his own State as a chain of commonwealths within commonwealths, each with its own surroundings and characteristics. It is the picture of these communes that may give permanence to the poem : —

" A hundred thousand right arms were lifted up on high,
　A hundred thousand voices sent back their loud reply ;
　Through the thronged towns of Essex the startling summons
　　rang,
　And up from bench and loom and wheel her young mechan-
　　ics sprang !

" The voice of free, broad Middlesex, — of thousands as of
　　one, —
　The shaft of Bunker calling to that of Lexington ;
　From Norfolk's ancient villages, from Plymouth's rocky
　　bound
　To where Nantucket feels the arms of ocean close her
　　round ;

"From rich and rural Worcester, where through the calm
　　repose
　Of cultured vales and fringing woods the gentle Nashua
　　flows,

To where Wachuset's wintry blasts the mountain larches
   stir,
Swelled up to Heaven the thrilling cry of 'God save Latimer!'

" And sandy Barnstable rose up, wet with the salt sea spray, —
   And Bristol sent her answering shout down Narragansett
      Bay!
Along the broad Connecticut old Hampden felt the thrill,
And the cheer from Hampshire's woodmen swept down from
      Holyoke Hill."

Whittier's position in these poems can only
be realized when we remember that of the
younger school of New England men of letters
he was virtually the only one who had given himself up to the cause of abolition. Longfellow
wrote his gentle and picturesque " Poems on
Slavery " in a few days in 1842, in the confine-
ment of a sea voyage, moved thereto by a chapter in Dickens's " American Notes." Bryant
held anti-slavery opinions, but he kept aloof from
the ardent reformers, and certainly did not overwhelm his muse with humanitarian politics.
Holmes was occupied with his profession. Hawthorne was living an intense and solitary inner
life, undisturbed by the tumult of the world.
Emerson early sympathized with the anti-slavery
movement in essence, but his interest was long
somewhat coldly philosophic. As he himself
said, he liked best " the strong and worthy persons who support the social order without hesi-

tation or misgiving. I like these; they never incommode us by exciting grief, pity, or perturbation of any sort. But the professed philanthropists, it is strange and horrible to say, are an altogether odious set of people, whom one would shun as the worst of bores and canters." [1] Like a philosopher, too, he saw below the surface of the agitation, and, realizing that mere emancipation was not all that was necessary to set matters right, he would have trusted much to time and to progress in civilization. It was not until the time of the fugitive slave agitations that he woke from his trance and took an active interest in anti-slavery politics, in some respects becoming quite naturally an extremist, as was shown by his attitude towards John Brown.

Lowell, drawn into the reform movement by his high-minded young wife, had for some time close relations with the abolitionists. In his class-poem of 1838 he had satirized them, — and Carlyle and Emerson into the bargain, — but in 1843 he wrote of Whittier in the "Pioneer" as "the fiery Koerner of his spiritual warfare, who, Scævola-like, has sacrificed on the altar of duty that right hand which might have made him acknowledged as the most passionate lyrist of his time." In 1845 he was at Philadelphia,

[1] J. E. Cabot, *A Memoir of Ralph Waldo Emerson* (1888), ii. 426.

writing editorials for Whittier's old paper,
the "Pennsylvania Freeman;" and in 1848–49
he was corresponding editor of the "National
Anti-Slavery Standard." In 1844 and 1845 he
wrote his spirited "Rallying Cry for New England" and "Another Rallying Cry by a Yankee," both in emulation of Whittier, and in 1846
he began his "Biglow Papers." Lowell as a
reformer was undoubtedly sincere; but he was
young, with high thoughts and a mind undisci-
plined by study or experience. His reform period was a transient phase of his life, and his
interest in abolition was neither so narrow nor
so intense as that of Whittier. He was devoted
rather to the general cause of humanitarianism
than to abolition, and, as his instincts for pure
letters grew stronger, he followed his bent. It
is interesting, however, to contrast his "Biglow
Papers" with Whittier's political poems. Whittier, the barefooted farmer's lad who milked
cows and hoed potatoes, who until he grew up
had lived on a lonely farm, Whittier the "peas-
ant" used the language he had always heard
and spoken, a pure English speech, with few
dialectic peculiarities. Lowell, brought up in the
outskirts of the city and in the company of
scholars and "gentlemen," built up for himself
a literary rustic dialect which no countryman,
if he used it at all, would have used when deal-

ing with matters of importance. Whittier, a rustic himself and writing for rustics in the usual literary forms, was read widely by them, and became a power throughout the North. Lowell, by adopting the artificial rustic form, cut himself off very largely from a rustic audience and influenced only city or literary folk. But, strange paradox again, Whittier's literary verses, though more effective, were less lasting, and Lowell's rustic verses have passed into literature.

In 1835 Whittier was thought of as a promising young lyricist of the Byronic type, who was beginning to be interested in reform; but such had been his ardor that by 1850 he was generally thought of only as an exuberant abolitionist versifier : —

> " Ah, Whittier ! Fighting Friend ! I like thy verse —
> Thy wholesale blessing and thy wholesale curse;
> I prize the spirit which exalts thy strain,
> And joy when truth impels thy blows amain;
> But, really, friend ! I cannot help suspecting,
> Though writing 's good, there 's merit in correcting !

> " Whittier, adieu ! my blows I would not spare,
> For when I strike, I strike who best can bear;
> Oft in this rhyme of mine I lash full hard
> The man whom much I love, as friend and bard;
> Even as the leech, inspired by science pure,
> Albeit he probe and cauterize — must cure ! "[1]

[1] *Parnassus in Pillory. A Satire.* By Motley Manners, Esq. New York, 1851.

Even Lowell, while recognizing Whittier's patriotism in cutting himself completely away from
the natural line of his development, implied that
the process was complete. In a laudatory review
of his collected poems in the " National Anti-
Slavery Standard " for December 21, 1848,
Lowell is inclined to ignore Whittier's poems on
other subjects than reform, praising him for the
essentially Yankee flavor of his verse, but depre-
cating his attempt to treat local themes — what
is the red man to us who are citizens of the
world ? — a criticism characteristic of the Cambridge school of thought, whose aim was rather to
Europeanize America than to aid it in its search
for individual expression. And again, in the
" Fable for Critics," written in the same year, he
puts entirely aside the non-humanitarian poems,
and dwells alone on Whittier's zeal as a reformer.

" Our Quaker leads off metaphorical fights
  For reform and whatever they call human rights,
  Both singing and striking in front of the war,
  And hitting his foes with the mallet of Thor ;
  Anne haec, one exclaims, on beholding his knocks,
  Vestis filii tui, O leather-clad Fox ?
  Can that be thy son, in the battle's mad din,
  Preaching brotherly love and then driving it in
  To the brain of the tough old Goliah of sin,
  With the smoothest of pebbles from Castaly's spring
  Impressed on his hard moral sense with a sling ? "

With our present ideas about the comparative
impermanency of Whittier's abolitionist poetry

and the greater lasting power of certain other parts of his work, it is hard to see how the general public could have so concentrated its attention on a single element in his verse, prominent though it was, to the exclusion of all else. And yet a glance at the published volumes of the period we are considering will confirm the contemporary judgment. "Lays of my Home" (1843) revealed other elements only in embryo; and "Voices of Freedom" (1846), "Poems" (1849), "Songs of Labor" (1850), "The Chapel of the Hermits" (1853), "The Panorama" (1856), though containing these elements in a more advanced form, did not reveal them in their full power.

We must, however, now stop to trace the growth of these half-concealed lines of development, which were to approach maturity in the fifties and in a later period were to give him fame of a new sort.

It is clear at the outset that Whittier's interest in reform extended beyond the limits of the abolitionist cause. His heart pleaded for the cause of the oppressed abroad as well as at home. His voice cheered on whoever fought for intellectual or industrial liberty, and rebuked those who wilfully ground their brethren beneath their feet. His ideal was the old ideal of the Puritans — purified and enlarged : —

" The riches of the Commonwealth
    Are free, strong minds, and hearts of health;
    And more to her than gold or grain,
    The cunning hand and cultured brain.

" For well she keeps her ancient stock,
    The stubborn strength of Pilgrim Rock;
    And still maintains, with milder laws,
    And clearer light, the Good Old Cause." [1]

As a Quaker Puritan should be, he was, though
tolerant in religious matters, a foe to the Roman
Catholic Church of the time on its social side.
He praised the German liberal Johannes Ronge
(" Strike home, strong-hearted man "), and de-
nounced Pius the Ninth : —

" Yet, Scandal of the World ! from thee
    One needful truth mankind shall learn :
    That kings and priests to Liberty
    And God are false in turn."

His natural fluency in verse, increased by years
of practice, and now controlled by the insight
acquired in years of active political experience,
made these poems of invective, if so they may
be styled, particularly powerful. They have the
orator's ringing tone, the politician's sense of
the essentially weak points in the adversary's
armor, the poet's skill of phrase, and his art in
stimulating the emotions. He had read widely,
and was quick to modify his native style by

[1] *Our State.*

adopting something of the tone of others, as is shown by the plain touch of Browning in his splendid " From Perugia : " —

> " Off with hats, down with knees, shout your vivas like mad !
>   Here 's the Pope in his holiday righteousness clad,
>   From shorn crown to toe-nail, kiss-worn to the quick,
>   Of sainthood in purple the pattern and pick,
>   Who the rôle of the priest and the soldier unites,
>   And, praying like Aaron, like Joshua fights."

In the second place, he was now so far removed from his old Byronic period, so purged of his immature pessimism and rebellion against the will of God, so changed from his boyish vanity and self-seeking, that the world took on a new meaning to him. Its outward vesture he was never skilled in portraying : his "nature" poems leave the senses unstirred. But he knew the hearts of earnest men, their despondencies, their aspirations ; and advancing age and his Quaker faith, now strong within him, were leading him to give to the quietism, to the renunciation to which the eager soul must finally attain, an expression which they had not had before in America. In this period neither the idea nor the expression was yet perfect, but one feels the power of both : —

> " Know well, my soul, God's hand controls
>   Whate'er thou fearest ;
>   Round Him in calmest music rolls
>   Whate'er thou hearest.

" What to thee is shadow, to Him is day,
    And the end He knoweth,
And not on a blind and aimless way
    The spirit goeth." [1]

It was not Calvinism that he thus sang, nor any
creed of any church, but the old mystery of the
Holy Spirit, inherent in many a religion and
perhaps to be confirmed by modern psychology
as the essence of religious life, — that strange
turning inward of the mind, beyond the limits
of the merely cognitive faculties, to that sub-
stratum of the spirit where the world and the
individual are most at one : —

" I turn from Fancy's cloud-built scheme,
    Dark creed, and mournful eastern dream
    Of power, impersonal and cold,
    Controlling all, itself controlled,
    Maker and slave of iron laws,
    Alike the subject and the cause;
    From vain philosophies, that try
    The sevenfold gates of mystery,
    And, baffled ever, babble still,
    Word-prodigal of fate and will;
    From Nature, and her mockery, Art,
    And book and speech of men apart." [2]

This beneficent process of mental and spiritual adjustment to the world — parallel to the
marvellous physiological process by which the
conservative forces replace diseased tissue and
conquer toxic influences — was also the cause of
the heightened tenderness that is observable in

[1] *My Soul and I.*   [2] *Questions of Life.*

the class of verses which he himself classed as
" subjective and reminiscent." Keen and far-
sighted as he was in practical affairs, his temperament was deeply emotional; a man of
moods, unmarried, without intimate friendships,
isolated, ill, without the supporting staff of a
business or professional routine, his thoughts
(and too often his poems) turned upon himself.
In the intervals of his preoccupation with politics, he fell into introspection : —

> " Life's mystery wrapt him like a cloud;
> He heard far voices mock his own,
> The sweep of wings unseen, the loud,
> Long roll of waves unknown." [1]

And introspection brought first that sense of
disappointment and almost of bereavement that
sounds now and then through his verse, — "the
bitter longings of a vain regret," — and then the
tender idealization of the early years in which
his hopes were still unbroken. As a bachelor,
he naturally found his fancies straying back to
the might-have-beens of his youth, to his boyish
affections for country lassies, of whom we may
guess there were two, one a more constant companion, recalled in " Memories " and " Benedicite," and one less familiarly known, but more
beloved, whose miniature and whose memory he
always cherished. The latter, as age advanced,

[1] *My Namesake.*

apparently became for him more of a Beatrice, but his mood was now to dream of the old childhood days with the former : —

> " Fair Nature's book together read,
>   The old wood-paths that knew our tread,
>   The maple shadows overhead, —
>
> " The hills we climbed, the river seen
>   By gleams along its deep ravine, —
>   All keep thy memory fresh and green. . . .
>
> " God's love and peace be with thee, where
>   Soe'er this soft autumnal air
>   Lifts the dark tresses of thy hair ! " [1]

The mood of reminiscence went further still, revisualizing, typifying, idealizing the whole field of old childish memories, — the barefoot days, the district-school days, — all full of sunshine and joy, but all with the touch of pathos that comes from the contrast between the *might-have-been* and the *is*. The public, itself grown out of the old simple life, was in the mood to indulge in such recollections. It first tasted that pleasure in " To My Old Schoolmaster " (1851), and more especially in " The Barefoot Boy " (1855), which was less local in its interests, and which furnished the type a few years later for Whittier's most famous piece of verse.

A still further development of importance in

---

[1] *Benedicite.*

this period was his growing skill in narrative verse. In the 1848 review Lowell had spoken slightingly of Whittier's Indian subjects, and with reason. After many experiments Whittier was compelled to give them up; he never caught the Indian mood, the primitive outlook. But their place was filled not with European legends, as was mainly the case with others, but with those of colonial days — the *magnalia* of the Puritan settlers, whose outlook he understood better than any other poet. He read much in old books and old records, and, pondering much on these things, began to recast fragments of the antique narratives, to enlarge and embellish the familiar incidents. Sometimes he merely polished and reset a quaint gem, as in "The Prophecy of Samuel Sewall," or commented wittily on a superstition, as in "The Double-Headed Snake of Newbury," or retold a fact or a legend that had a point of piety, as in "The Exiles," "Cassandra Southwick," "The Garrison of Cape Ann," and "The Swan Song of Parson Avery;" or took a poet's liberty in inventing supposedly typical incidents, as in "Mary Garvin" and "Mabel Martin." He wrote less than a score of these narrative poems in a period covering as many years, but they are all excellent and grow better with time, for they were based on knowledge and sympathy, and though perhaps quickly written, embody material long assimilated and individualized.

Three poems belonging to this general group, "Skipper Ireson's Ride," "The Telling of the Bees," and "Maud Muller," are indeed among his very best, and represent the highest degree of skill in localized narrative that has yet been attained in American poetry. These are less antique in subject, and two of them have no basis in fact. After his long studies in drawing, as it were, from historical figures, Whittier was prepared to compose for himself a typical incident, instead of culling it from the records of the past. "Skipper Ireson's Ride" was built around the burden of a half-remembered old Marblehead ballad, and though false to the facts of the actual incident, is ideally true to the life of that rough and strange old town, in Whittier's days, and almost to our own, as isolated, as individual, as picturesque in speech and custom and outward air as a remote fishing village of the English or Brittany coast. It is a real ballad, strong of the soil, born of familiar acquaintance, not, like Longfellow's "Wreck of the Hesperus," so imperfectly localized that the author had only the vaguest notion where lay his reef of Norman's Woe; and yet we must not forget that the verses were originally written without the dialectic refrain, and that it is to

Lowell's good sense that we owe the change. In " Telling the Bees " Whittier comes nearest to the art of Tennyson or Browning, and it is plain that in writing it he had the latter's work in mind ; the matter is slight, the development in lyric rather than in narrative form, the method restrained, the effect delicate.   Its unusual tone and manner make it less typical of Whittier, and it is not so well known as many poems less good.   I mention it here, however, to call attention both to the element of imitation in his verse and to his skill in the handling of an unfamiliar form.   But the greatest favorite of all was " Maud Muller," probably his most effective piece of purely narrative poetry, for it went at once to the hearts of the people, and, almost in spite of the critics, has retained its place there.   It is very simple verse, so unpretentious in form that it is now thought almost commonplace, so unsophisticated, so rural in its philosophy that it is often actually despised.   And yet nothing could ring truer, or lie closer to the heart of the communities of the old Northern democracy, than Whittier's doctrine here and elsewhere that instinctive love is the natural guide, worth the real test, social " position " a negligible quantity.   It is obvious that a part of the effect of the poem is due to the fact that simple-hearted folks feel this doctrine to be true, and hence recognize the pathos of Whittier's illustrative incident. But the real cause lies deeper still. It is the "might have been" that is the familiar quotation. What has impressed the people at large so tremendously must be, not the fact of convention directing affection, not the *must-not-be* or the *could-not-have-been*, but the *might-have-been*, and that not merely in matters of love but in all ultimate and essential aims of human ambition. Theoretically, we are happily placed in a land where social rank scarcely exists and opportunity lies open to all. No hard barrier of convention keeps us from success. No rule governs, no custom prescribes, only chance controls — and guides blindly. In a complete democracy, more than elsewhere, the *may-be* is the great joy of youth, and the *might-have-been* the subtle regret of age.

All the while Whittier was writing prose, clear, solid, and instructive prose, of the sort that added to his reputation with the public and increased his own power as a man, a thinker, and a poet. We often forget the sound basis of information on which a poet's skill must rest until our attention is in some way called to the breadth of his reading or to the extent of his experience. To read Whittier's prose is to see this sub-structure of his verse.

Of his work as a political journalist we have already spoken. Besides this he contributed general articles and critical reviews to his own and to other papers, and it was matter of this kind which he furnished to the " National Era " from 1847 to 1860, sometimes to the extent of five or six columns a week. Some of these articles he collected[1] from time to time in little books: " The Stranger in Lowell " (1845), " The Supernaturalism of New England " (1847), "Leaves from Margaret Smith's Journal " (1849), " Old Portraits and Modern Sketches " (1850), and " Literary Recreations and Miscellanies "(1854).

The sketches that compose " The Stranger in Lowell " were published in the " Middlesex Standard " during his brief period of editorship,

---

[1] Among the many minor articles which have not been reprinted I find two passages of interest : —

" Our poetry is cold — abstract — imitative — the labor of overtasked and jaded intellects, rather than the spontaneous outgushing of hearts warm with love, and strongly sympathizing with human nature as it actually exists about us — with the joys and griefs, the good and even the ill of our common humanity." (September 9, 1847.)

" He [Lowell] is yet a young man, and, in view of what he has already attained, we have a right to expect a good deal of his future. May he have strength and long life to do for freedom and humanity, and for the true and permanent glory of American literature, all that others less gifted and subject to less favorable circumstances have strived in vain to accomplish." (January 17, 1850.)

and most of them have been included in his collected works. His preface explains their origin :
" Occupying, during a brief sojourn in Lowell
the past autumn, a position which necessarily
brought him into somewhat harsh collision with
both of the great political parties on the eve of
an exciting election, he [the author] deemed it
at once a duty and a privilege to keep his heart
open to the kindliest influences of nature and
society. These pages are a transcript — too free
and frank perhaps — of impressions made upon
his mind by the common incidents of daily life."
Written, as he confesses, " without plan or co-
herence, penned in the intervals of severer and
more earnest labors, often under circumstances
of bodily illness and suffering," these sketches
are not a guide to the town or a sociological
treatise on it. But they reveal in a charming
way the characteristics of a New England manufacturing city in its early days, when the working people there were largely of native origin,
when this novel mechanical toil was a great boon
to women of little or no means, when laborers
had strength and ambition to cultivate their
minds, and when such a community had still
in it an almost Utopian freshness and vigor.
Whittier praised the women and the not ex-
hausting labor, was delighted at the picturesque influx of other nationalities, and noted

significantly that here " work is the patron saint.
Everything bears his image and superscription.
Here is no place for that respectable class of
citizens called gentlemen, and for their much
vilified brethren familiarly known as loafers."
It is from this testimony and from the corresponding evidence in Lucy Larcom's " A New
England Girlhood " that we can reconstruct the
days when the old New England virtues were
holding their own in the as yet unrealized struggle with the ills of industrial centralization.

" The Supernaturalism of New England " is
likewise of value to the student of the old New
England life. It attempted to embrace, so far
as the author's reading and experience permitted
him, " the present superstitions and still current
traditions of New England, in the hope that . . .
it may hereafter furnish material for the essay-
ist and the poet who shall one day do for our
own native land what Scott and Hogg and
Burns and Wilson have done for theirs." He
includes all incidents which would nowadays be
investigated by a psychical research society, and
intimates that the whole subject is worth further
study ; and though it is plain that he holds his
judgment in reserve, he finds, beneath " the
exaggeration and distortion of actual fact, a
great truth : " " it is Nature herself repelling
the slanders of the materialist, and vindicating

her claim to an informing and all-directing Spirit." As an example of his pleasant prose style, and as an illustration of the influences that surrounded him as a child, I may be allowed to quote the following incident: —

"Whoever has seen Great Pond, in the East parish of Haverhill, has seen one of the very loveliest of the thousand little lakes or ponds of New England. With its soft slopes of greenest verdure, its white and sparkling sand-rim, its southern hem of pine and maple, mirrored, with spray and leaf, in the glassy water, its graceful hill-sentinels round about, white with the orchard-bloom of spring, or tasselled with the corn of autumn, its long sweep of blue waters, broken here and there by picturesque headlands, it would seem a spot of all others where spirits of evil must shrink, rebuked and abashed, from the presence of the Beautiful. Yet here, too, has the shadow of the supernatural fallen. A lady of my acquaintance, a staid, unimaginative church-member, states that a few years ago she was standing in the angle formed by the two roads, one of which traverses the pond shore, the other leading over the hill which rises abruptly from the water. It was a warm summer evening, just at sunset. She was startled by the appearance of a horse and cart of the kind used a century ago in New England, driving rapidly down the steep hillside, and crossing the wall a few yards before her, without noise, or the displacing of a stone. The driver sat sternly erect, with a fierce countenance, grasping the reins tightly, and looking neither to the right nor the left. Behind the cart, and apparently lashed to it, was a woman of gigantic size, her countenance convulsed with a blended expression of rage and agony, writhing and struggling, like Laocoön in the folds of the serpent. Her head, neck, feet, and arms were naked; wild locks of gray hair streamed back from temples corrugated and darkened. The horrible cavalcade swept by across the street, and disappeared at the margin of the pond."

"Leaves from Margaret Smith's Journal in the Province of Massachusetts Bay" is, like the two preceding volumes, a study of New England conditions; but this, more than the others, overwhelms us with the minuteness of its antiquarian lore and with its philosophic and scholarly grasp of the subject. Whittier knew the life of the Commonwealth as Scott knew that of the Border; and at a time when most students of New England history were mere apologists for the queer old theocracy, he was both acute enough to see through the sham and wise enough not to be blinded by the prejudice of reaction. His isolation and his Quakerhood both helped him. He

was unaffected by the modern impulse to glorify
the period of origin; he saw the Massachusetts
of the seventeenth century as his pioneer ancestor might have seen it, or that ancestor's old
neighbor, Robert Pike, and not as Cotton
Mather or Ward of Agawam saw it. The plot is
slight. Margaret Smith, fresh from England,
and related to important folk among the settlers,
meets the chief people in the Massachusetts Bay
Colony, journeys to Newbury and further east
to Agamenticus, and afterwards to the heretical
colony in Rhode Island, seeing everywhere the
famous old worthies, — Saltonstalls, Mathers,
Sewalls, Eliots, Wards, Pikes, and Wiggles-
worths. She describes the bright landscape and
the strenuous pioneer life with almost as much
vividness as Defoe might have done; she sees the
arrogant priesthood smelling out witchcraft and
hunting down heresy; the pathetic dispossessed
Indian; the simple-minded Quakers, goaded into
an hysterical fanaticism; the earnest colonists,
also simple-hearted, and at bottom, we may sur-
mise, not too religious, though priest-ridden, and
keeping alive their ancestral love of fair play,
of order and frugality, of freedom and toleration, of plain common sense mingled with energy
and aspiration — virtues that, as the power of
the hierarchy was slowly broken, were to become
the real source of the greatness of New England.

The book will never be widely read. It is too slight in substance, too sober in style. But no single modern volume could be found which has so penetrated the secret of colonial times in Massachusetts, for it is, almost line by line, a transcript and imaginative interpretation of old letters, journals, and memoirs. There is scarcely a passage in it that is not based on a given document, scarcely a seeming fancy that is not closely paralleled by fact.

" Old Portraits and Modern Sketches " was a collection of ten little essays which had previously appeared in the " National Era," seven of which deal with such old worthies as Bunyan and Ellwood. The remaining three are on the abolitionists, William Leggett and Nathaniel P. Rogers, both of whom had recently died, and on the Windham farmer and versifier, Robert Dinsmore, — a charming little essay, to which I called attention in connection with Whittier's boyish admiration for Burns. These articles show no special research, but they are far from commonplace, and they deserve to be read more often than they are. Their two striking characteristics, revealing Whittier's taste and temper, are an absence of literary allusion and a praiseworthy unwillingness to generalize. Strictly speaking, Whittier did not care much for literature. He loved men and things and books of biography and travel; he liked to know how the world looked and what brave spirits had wrought in it. Toward fiction and fanciful poetry he does not seem, in his maturity, to have been strongly drawn; and he was constitutionally averse to creating philosophic theories about life or letters. These traits, which differentiate him from Lowell and Emerson, give his essays a marked sobriety and actuality of tone, which limit their range and their effectiveness, but which have for the attentive reader a special and individual charm.

"Literary Recreations and Miscellanies" contains much matter from "The Stranger in Lowell" and from "The Supernaturalism of New England," and about a dozen fresh studies, which had also appeared in the "National Era," on New England antiquities, of which the essay on the "Great Ipswich Fright" is typical. It contains also several articles of literary criticism, which throw fresh light on Whittier's reading and his sound judgment. He was not a learned reader, like Lowell, nor a philosophic reader, like Emerson, nor indeed a wide reader in pure literature, like Longfellow. But these few essays, as well as his correspondence, the testimony of his friends, and the books on his shelves, show him to have been a man of very considerable information, and capable of giving sound judgment on good literature. He recognized the merits of Macaulay's History without being too much repelled or attracted by its rhetoric. He was pardonably indignant at Carlyle's " Occasional Discourse on the Negro Question," a certain fundamental justness in which he was less able than we are to appreciate, and which he thought took " issue with the moral sense of mankind and the precepts of Christianity." He recognized the value of Bayard Taylor's works. He liked Dr. Holmes's verse ("a merry doctor!"). He welcomed Longfellow's " Evangeline:" — " Eureka! Here, then, we have it at last, — an American poem, with the lack of which British reviewers have so long reproached us." In the old-fashioned manner which became him so well, he took, too, the liberty of departing speedily from the book in question, to discourse on the ideas which it suggested. In the case of " Evangeline," which had been his subject as well as Hawthorne's before Longfellow took it up, he was drawn at once into a consideration of the mingling virtues and vices in the old New England Puritanism, the closing passage of which is worth quoting here as another admirable illustration of his own tolerance of spirit and keenness of mental vision : —

" Of all that is noble and true in the Puritan character we are sincere admirers. The generous and self-denying apostleship of Eliot is, of itself, a beautiful page in their history. The physical daring and hardihood with which, amidst the times of savage warfare, they laid the foundations of mighty states, and subdued the rugged soil, and made the wilderness blossom ; their steadfast adherence to their religious principles, even when the Restoration had made apostasy easy and profitable ; and the vigilance and firmness with which, under all circumstances, they held fast their chartered liberties and extorted new rights and privileges from the reluctant home government, — justly entitle them to the grateful remembrance of a generation now reaping the fruits of their toils and sacrifices. But in expressing our gratitude to the founders of New England, we should not forget what is due to truth and justice ; nor, for the sake of vindicating them from the charge of that religious intolerance which, at the time, they shared with nearly all Christendom, undertake to defend, in the light of the nineteenth century, opinions and practices hostile to the benignant spirit of the gospel and subversive of the inherent rights of man."

Such was Whittier's product in verse and in prose during the long middle period of his life, — a period less important in its actual results than it was potentially, for he was still identified in the public mind with abolitionism, and much of his best work was yet to be done. It was for the most part a period of disappointment, weakness, and hardship, and his prevailing mood seems to have been indicated in this letter to " Grace Greenwood : " —

" 5th mo., 10, 1849.

" We have had a dreary spring — a gray haze in the sky — a dim, beam-shorn sun — a wind from the northeast, cold as if sifted through all the ices of frozen Labrador, as terrible almost as that chill wind which the old Moslem fable says will blow over the earth in the last days. The birds hereabout have a sorry time of it, as well as ' humans.' There are now, however, indications of a change for the better. The blossoms of the peach and cherry are just opening, and the arbutus, anemones, and yellow violets are making glad and beautiful the banks of our river. I feel daily like thanking God for the privilege of looking upon another spring. I have written very little this spring, — the 'Legend of St. Mark' is all in the line of verse that I have attempted. I feel a growing disinclination to pen and ink. Overworked and tired by the long weary years of the anti-slavery struggle, I want mental rest. I have already lived a long life, if thought and action constitute

it. I have crowded into a few years what should
have been given to many." [1]

But the late summer of his life was slowly
opening. The accumulative power of his narrative and reminiscent verse was impressing the
people, and his poetry began to be remunerative.
In 1849 B. B. Mussey and Company of Boston
paid him five hundred dollars for the copyrights
of all his verse hitherto issued, and published his
collected poems in a handsome volume, on which
he received a royalty and which passed into a
third edition. At about the same time James T.
Fields, whom Whittier had known for some
years, began his connection with the publishing
house of Mr. Ticknor. He had a hearty, genial
personality, and a genuine and fairly acute taste
for literature, a taste which was then rare in that
perilous field of enterprise where many fail and
few prosper, and only those succeed in publishing
books that are both good and remunerative who
have, as a sort of sixth sense, an appreciation for
the essentials of real literature which is almost
as great as the genius of the poet or the novelist.
Fields drew Whittier with him and found the best
in him, and from 1850 on Whittier's new books
were published by the Ticknor firm, which finally
purchased Mussey's rights and issued the blue
and gold volumes of Whittier's collected poems

[1] Pickard, *Life*, i. 335.

in 1857. Under such good management, his royalties grew larger and the long pressure of poverty began to be relaxed.

Friends and acquaintances in abundance Whittier had always had, brothers-in-arms in the cause of reform, political and religious, and colleagues, neighbors, and townsmen; but his companions both by choice and necessity were almost always simple rural folks, unknown to fame now or then, but righteous, sturdy souls, to whom he justly gave due honor. Like the typical New Englander, who is in essence a man of the sea-coast village or the hill hamlet, he opened his heart to few or none, and lived the old life of reticence and privacy, so foreign to town and city ways. City people, indeed, he seems to have thought of as a slightly different breed of men, perhaps slightly to be distrusted. With Holmes, at that period, he had no acquaintance, and with Longfellow he was always on terms of formality; Emerson he knew a little better, but not at all well. Hawthorne he seems scarcely to have met. With Lowell he had been brought into relations by their common anti-slavery interests. They wrote to each other without much restraint as occasion demanded, but nothing like intimacy existed between them. Whittier was a member of the Saturday Club of the Boston circle of authors, and he was one of the charter members, so to speak, of the "Atlantic" group. He was in correspondence with Sumner, Hale, and other men of political importance. Beecher and Phillips supped with him at the Amesbury cottage and lectured for him at the Amesbury Lyceum. In 1858 he was elected an overseer of Harvard College. He was becoming a man of national distinction, and his social and intellectual position was secure. But in city life he appeared rarely and reluctantly, partly on account of ill health, largely from preference; and in his letters to men of affairs and men of letters alike the tone of genuine affection is missing. An exception must perhaps be made in the case of Sumner, and certainly in the case of Bayard Taylor, whose genius he early recognized, and towards whom he was drawn from the first. The letters that passed between them are tokens of a warm though probably by no means an intimate friendship, and they enjoyed their infrequent meetings. Taylor wrote to a friend, July 22, 1850 : — "Friday morning early, Lowell and I started for Amesbury, which we reached in a terrible northeaster. What a capital time we had with Whittier, in his nook of a study, with the rain pouring on the roof, and the wind howling at the door!" In the main, however, Whittier led a secluded and a lonely life. It was natural to his individual temperament and to his emotional inheritance.

It was, moreover, the source of his power as a poët. Only the pure mind, unstained by passion, only the solitary heart, given over to meditation, was capable of throwing over the simple farming life a reminiscent glamour of boyish romance.

CHAPTER VI

WHITTIER's direct and formal connection with the main body of abolitionists had ceased about 1840, in consequence of his determination to stand by the lesser body, the " new organization," of which he was one of the leaders, in its desire to build up a third political party. The line of advance of this body naturally became a result-ant, a series of compromises and adjustments for the sake of ultimately securing the end in view. That end was secured; but long before that the formal " new organization " had disappeared and its members had become participants in the vari-ous political movements that led to the formation of the Republican party. The " old organiza-tion " held itself intact to the last, and even, under the direction of Wendell Phillips, tried to maintain itself, after the adoption of the Thir-teenth Amendment, as an instrument for secur-ing the political equality of the negro. But Garrison, who had not shifted his course by a fraction of a point since the establishment of the

"Liberator" in 1831, closed the career of that journal at the passage of the amendment. It was then a fit time for all men to unite in praising the constancy to their great cause of the abolitionist chiefs and their followers, and such internal differences of opinion as had existed among the agitators were lost in the common rejoicing over their victory in establishing their main principle. Garrison and Whittier exchanged affectionate letters on more than one occasion. Garrison was glad to pay honor to his old friend and co-worker, in spite of their divergent views as to the means to be employed in their crusade. In 1865, when Garrison's fellow-townsmen of Newburyport congratulated him on the triumphant culmination of his life work, and formally celebrated his visit to his birthplace, Whittier wrote a hymn for the services in the city hall; and in 1863, at the time of the commemoration of the thirtieth anniversary of the formation of the American Anti-Slavery Society, he concluded his formal letter of reminiscence, written for publication, with this open statement of his long-continued affection : "For thyself, I need not say that the love and esteem of early boyhood have lost nothing by the test of time." Thus, by kindly and fraternal words on both sides, the breach was closed, and the biographer has the satisfaction of recording the complete reconciliation of those two noble men, whose lives and work have been so strangely intermingled.

With the growth of anti-slavery opinion in the North that marked the close of the compromise period, and with the birth of the new party, Whittier's active share in politics decreased. The cause of anti-slavery, however, remained the great interest of his life. As a Quaker and as a believer in reform by legal means, he deprecated John Brown's wild attempt to kindle the flames of rebellion, and though in the main an upholder of the Union, he was horror-stricken by the war. He followed Sumner in his opposition to Seward's attempts at a last compromise, but he would almost have preferred dissolution to the terrible alternative, and he had to the last a feeling — in which his usual sagacity was absent — that somehow the trial by arms could then be avoided: —

" For myself, I would like to maintain the Union if it could be *the* Union of our fathers. But if it is to be in name only ; if the sacrifices and concessions upon which it lives must all be made by the Free States to the Slave; if the peaceful victories of the ballot-box are to be turned into defeats by threats of secession ; if rebellion and treason are to be encouraged into a standing menace, a power above law and Constitution, demanding perpetual sacrifice, I, for one, shall not lift a hand against its dissolution.

As to fighting, in any event, to *force back* the
seceders, I see no sense in it. Let them go on
with their mad experiment, the government simply holding its own, and enforcing its revenue
laws, until this whole matter can be fairly submitted to the people for their final adjudication."[1]

The war once begun, his principles did not
allow him to approve it nor to aid the belliger-
ents he thought to be fighting for the right: he
could only wait the outcome with anxious sorrow.
But he continually urged that slavery was the
real point at issue, and in his correspondence with
men of authority and influence in the United
States and in England, he helped to keep the
vital question at the front. In the matter of
reconstruction he held to Sumner's extreme doctrine.

The main interest in Whittier's life was politics rather than literature, and it could not be
expected that this interest would die away when
the cause to which he devoted himself had tri-
umphed. He still watched the affairs of the
state and the nation, and gave counsel freely, as
befitted one grown old in political service. He
exerted himself to counteract the bitter feeling
against Sumner which arose after his attack on
Grant's administration in 1872; and he was
foremost in the persistent effort that resulted

[1] Pickard, *Life*, ii. 436.

in annulling the Massachusetts resolutions of censure against him for his proposition that the names of battles in the Civil War should not be borne on the flags of national regiments. He urged the education of the negro and the Indian ; he praised Gordon, soldier though he was; he interested himself in various minor causes; he wrote in commendation or in suggestion to prominent government officials and to great politicians; he was consulted in district and state affairs. Too old to change his vote when the reaction against the Republicans set in, he yet felt the force of the counter movement and respected its best motives. Long a partisan, he became in his later years a lover of the right irrespective of party, a friend of freedom and truth and honest dealing under any name.

In word as well as in deed Whittier's share in the anti-slavery conflict grew less. It had passed beyond the phase in which his pen or his counsel could aid. As long as the strife was one of intellect and emotion, and the appeal was to the judgment and the ballot, his verses were powerful instruments in the bloodless strife. But now that the passions of men were aflame, the Quaker's lips were dumb. His old stinging satire flashed out for an instant, at need, when, to use his own words of years later, " in the stress of our terrible war, the English ruling class, with few exceptions, were either coldly indifferent or hostile to the party of freedom." But this was the only occasion where he could render such a service. His religion — stern in this precept only — kept him away from the strife, out of real sympathy with it, for to his creed the blood-stained triumph was scarcely a victory, though a defeat at arms would have been the worst punishment God could have visited upon his cause. His station was with the old men, the women, and the children, helpless, innocent, pathetically resigned to the woes which were not of their making and yet which engulfed them. The verses wrung from him in these bitter years were not the warrior's shout, but the wail of the stricken woman, the prayer of faith and resignation that breathed submission to the will of Heaven and trust in the outcome of the right. His poems in this vein, " Thy Will be Done " and " Ein Feste Burg ist Unser Gott," were thus the voice of a great multitude, and in this way he was still the spokesman of the North.

Indeed, the Friend was able, after a fashion, to speak even to the soldier in his grimmest mood. The desire he had above all others, he told one of the Hutchinson singers before the war, was to write verses that might be sung.[1] But the battle-hymn of a people is as rarely written by

[1] J. W. Hutchinson, *Story of the Hutchinsons* (1896), 397.

the man of genius as is the music to which it is sung. To catch the rhythm to which armies shall march, to find the simple tune that the men in the ranks must sing, to come upon the crude imagery which shall express the obscure, underlying, slowly evolving thought of a myriad multitude, is not the task for a lettered man. The wordless passion must spread from brain to brain until felt by the people at large, until its accumulated might utters itself spontaneously in some simple form on the lips of some obscure singer whom chance shall choose. Thus it was with "John Brown's body lies a-mouldering in the grave" and with "We're coming, Father Abraham, three hundred thousand more," and, indeed, with "Mine eyes have seen the glory of the coming of the Lord," — the mystical utterance of an excited woman, who scarcely knew what she wrote. But though Whittier could not make such songs, — no poet could or did, — "We wait beneath the furnace-blast" and other verses were sung to the Union soldiers by the Hutchinson family — strange band of minstrels before the Lord — and aroused great enthusiasm by their moral force. Especially strong was the effect of the stanza: —

> "What gives the wheat-field blades of steel?
>   What points the rebel cannon?
> What sets the roaring rabble's heel
>   On the old star-spangled pennon?

What breaks the oath
Of the men o' the South ?
What whets the knife
For the Union's life ? —
Hark to the answer : Slavery ! "

The army authorities were at first unwilling
to have such plain truths uttered, and the per-
mission given to the Hutchinsons was revoked.
But the matter was carried up to President
Lincoln, who read the poems to the Cabinet and
declared that those were the very songs he
wanted his soldiers to hear.

The poetry of any permanent value produced
by the war, both in the North and in the South,
is very small in quantity, and may perhaps be
regarded as virtually reducing itself to Whitman's " My Captain," Lowell's " Commemoration Ode," and Whittier's " Barbara Frietchie."
The first is possibly the greatest, in that it is the
most direct and spontaneous translation of the
emotion of a people into beautiful imagery ;
the second is the thoughtful exposition, by the
scholar and the statesman, of the national retrospect ; the third is the only ballad of the conflict, North or South, that has found its way to
the hearts of the people. The alleged facts on
which " Barbara Frietchie " was founded have
been somewhat hotly discussed ; but it is clear
that Whittier was guiltless of distorting in any
way the incident as it was reported to him, and

that, furthermore, whether the supposed incident
actually occurred or not is of no importance.   It
was rumored to have occurred, and the rumor
was accepted as a fitting image of a real and
great emotion of the people.   For the incident
and the poem are nothing but Webster's feder-
alist speeches put into ballad form, nothing but
a type of the great fact of common nationality
which both sections were forgetting.   The stars
and stripes seemed to the South to stand for unjust interference with the rights of certain states,
and it became to them, as to the Union army,
not the symbol of the country but only of the
North.   The gray-haired woman, herself a re-
minder of the epoch when sectional differences
did not exist, by her loyalty to the old standard
under circumstances where it was regarded only
as a hostile emblem, is thus the incarnation of
the honor due, both North and South, to the
banner of our fathers, an honor in these later
years now again paid throughout our land.   The
rebuke offered to the South was sectional in
its appeal ; it was unjust in its inference that
General Jackson was not acting a noble part in
his defence of his state.   But a popular ballad
cannot be delicate in its shading.   The " rebel "
leader must feel the blush of shame, just as he
must melodramatically order a company to shoot
at a flag, instead of quietly instructing a corporal

to have it removed. The power of the poem now, and its high significance then, lay not merely in its perfect form, but in the direction which it gave the thoughts of every reader toward the ideal of national unity.

As the burden of his political cause bore less heavily on his shoulders, Whittier turned with alacrity to his older moods, which, as he explains in the prelude to " The Tent on the Beach," he had all the while felt calling him : —

> " For while he wrought with strenuous will
>   The work his hands had found to do,
> He heard the fitful music still
>   Of winds that out of dream-land blew.
> The din about him could not drown
> What the strange voices whispered down ;
> Along his task-field weird processions swept,
> The visionary pomp of stately phantoms stepped.
>
> " The common air was thick with dreams, —
>   He told them to the toiling crowd ;
> Such music as the woods and streams
>   Sang in his ear he sang aloud ;
> In still, shut bays, on windy capes,
>   He heard the call of beckoning shapes,
> And, as the gray old shadows prompted him,
> To homely moulds of rhyme he shaped their legends grim."

The best poems of this last period are thus narrative or legendary or religious rather than political. Already an old man, he was destined to make his position in American poetry secure by a comparatively long period of devotion to

the ideals of his boyhood, achieving in his full-
ripened maturity with skill and success what he
had wrought at so blunderingly in his youth.

His narrative poems were somewhat influenced
in form by those of Longfellow, but differ distinctly from his in subject, Longfellow's shorter
pieces being much more frequently the retelling
of foreign rather than native tales. Whittier's
subjects, on the contrary, were by preference
American and New England. He loved Oriental
apologues, as befitted one who read travels
greedily and whose trend of thought was ethical, and was skilful in framing them; but he
dwelt with most affection on native legends and
was most successful in treating them. Here the
long studies of old days and his complete famil-
iarity with local history and tradition availed him
at last. The Indian reappears, not tricked out,
like Mogg Megone, in the style of Scott and
tinged with the mood of Byron; no longer an
active, struggling, dramatic creature, hated, war-
ring, and oppressed, but a mere phantom of
colonial days, softened by long retrospect, dim
memories of whom are awakened by aged mon-
uments, and whose harsh traits are subdued
by antiquity. The old Quaker figures reappear
— martyrs, protestants, and prophets — in the
" Pennsylvania Pilgrim " and in a number of
shorter poems. And they are joined by the

witches and their judges, the whole *dramatis
personæ* of the period of supernaturalism; by
seventeenth-century maidens and their lovers,
by soldiers like John Underhill, by Parson
Bachiler, and by the dim shadows of less well-
known folk, until the buried past rises, spectre-
like, to earth again.

In this ballad-making, as I have remarked,
Whittier owes much to Longfellow; for though
he was himself a pioneer in the field, he for a
time well-nigh deserted it, whereas Longfellow
came to it fresh from the narrative romances of
Europe and with abundant leisure. But in the
native ballad, when he returned to cultivate it,
Whittier far surpassed Longfellow in force and
in truth. Longfellow's eyes were turned Europe-
ward, and he wrote of his old land like a half-
familiar stranger. Whittier's smallest phrase is
accurately true to fact, to tradition, or to our
sense of the typical and probable. Beneath the
artistic form lies the firm skeleton of history, as
beneath the often fanciful Norse saga is plainly
to be felt the presence of actual locality, incident, and personality. He realized, too, like the
wise antiquary, the limitations of the colonial civilization, — its prejudice and cruelty, its crude-
ness and barrenness, — and he saw, in later
times, not only the sturdy descendants of the
old stock, but

"Shrill, querulous women, sour and sullen men,
 Untidy, loveless, old before their time,
 With scarce a human interest save their own
 Monotonous round of small economies,
 Or the poor scandal of the neighborhood." [1]

This group of narrative poems are all historical in character and moralizing in purpose save one, unique in Whittier's work, "Annie and Rhoda," which, as Mr. Higginson observes, bears a strong resemblance to the modern pseudo-mediæval ballads of Rossetti, and which, I may add, was probably composed under his influence, for the range and variety of Whittier's poetical experiments have not been sufficiently noted. Whittier was keen to see the elements of another's art and to enrich his own thereby. He profited not only by the models of his boyhood but — more slightly — by Tennyson, Browning, and Arnold; and it is pleasant to hear Rossetti's note of Old World supernaturalism echoed back in this grim ballad of Cape Ann, in which the maiden who has buried her affection in her heart sees the vision of the wrecked and lost fisherman and hears his cry, while his betrothed is blind to the sight and deaf to his words. It was not often that the reticent old Quaker, holding so closely to the fact, thus gave his fancy play.

[1] Prelude to *Among the Hills*.

Much interest, too, attaches to three narrative poems of this period, "The Maids of Attitash," "Among the Hills," and "Amy Wentworth," the last by far the most beautiful, all tracking back to the moral of "Maud Muller." They are indeed its companion pieces, showing the happy loves of those mated in affection, the happier for their disparity in wealth and social standing. It was Whittier's own heart that spoke here, prompted, no doubt, by his observation of the growing gulf created by various degrees of fortune between men and women who were by nature each other's best mates; and no social or ethical teaching of his is more needed in our own time than this true and democratic doctrine of his that the old stock must be grafted with the new, that

> "The stream is brightest at its spring,
>   And blood is not like wine;
> Nor honored less than he who heirs
>   Is he who founds a line."

Whittier's feeling on this point may be imagined to have some connection, however remote, with what we infer to have been his own experience — some love of his youth, it would appear, having lapsed because he was too plainly a poor farmer's lad. In the mood of reminiscence that grew more intense as his share in active life decreased, it would seem that his fancy dwelt

more and more on this, exaggerating in his
dreams the social distance between him and his
child-love. In "My Playmate," "The Henchman," the "Sea Dream," the same theme appears, dealt with more or less freely. He was
"the boy who fed her father's kine," and is still
a rustic, while "haply with her jewelled hands
she smooths her silken gown : " —

> " And still the pines of Ramoth wood
>   Are moaning like the sea, —
> The moaning of the sea of change
>   Between myself and thee ! "

And thus this country girl with the brown
hair, unseen for fifty years, became to the dear
old man his Beatrice, a transfigured being, the
image of all that might have been, the type of
joys unknown, the pure guide of his spirit, the
memory of a meeting with whom at Marblehead,
by "the gray fort's broken wall," was woven
into what is to me his most musical and most
lovely poem : —

> " Thou art not here, thou art not there,
>   Thy place I cannot see ;
> I only know that where thou art
>   The blessed angels be,
>   And heaven is glad for thee.

> " Forgive me if the evil years
>   Have left on me their sign ;
> Wash out, O soul so beautiful,

The many stains of mine
In tears of love divine!

" I could not look on thee and live,
If thou wert by my side;
The vision of a shining one,
The white and heavenly bride,
Is well to me denied.

" But turn to me thy dear girl-face
Without the angel's crown,
The wedded roses of thy lips,
Thy loose hair rippling down
In waves of golden brown.

" Look forth once more through space and time,
And let thy sweet shade fall
In tenderest grace of soul and form
On memory's frescoed wall,
A shadow, and yet all!

" Draw near, more near, forever dear!
Where'er I rest or roam,
Or in the city's crowded streets,
Or by the blown sea foam,
The thought of thee is home ! "

These verses of reminiscence, beautiful as
they are, are less widely known, and rightly so,
than " Snow-Bound," written when, his mother
and sister dead, the memory mood was strongest
in him, and generally judged to be his most characteristic poem.   It is so familiar to young and
old that it would be superfluous to describe it
or to analyze it in detail, but it is not improper

to dwell for a moment on three points concerning it.

First, it is marvellous to notice how the most special and personal facts of Whittier's individual experience, thus accurately stated, become typical of the experiences of all his New England fellows. Whittier was, from one point of view, a highly specialized local product. Like Lucy Larcom he might have wondered: "If I had opened my eyes upon this planet elsewhere than in this northeastern corner of Massachusetts, elsewhere than on this green, rocky strip of shore between Beverly Bridge and the Misery Islands, it seems to me as if I must have been somebody else, and not myself. These gray ledges hold me by the roots, as they do the bayberry bushes, the sweet-fern, and the rock-saxifrage." [1]

He, this old man who had been an East Haverhill boy, describes *his* homestead, *his* well-sweep, *his* brook, *his* family circle, *his* schoolmaster, apparently intent on naught but the complete accuracy of his narrative, and lo! such is his art that he has drawn the one perfect, imperishable picture of that bright old winter life in that strange clime. Diaries, journals, histories, biographies, and autobiographies, with the same aim in view, are not all together so

[1] *A New England Girlhood.*

typical as this unique poem of less than a thousand lines.

Second, this generalizing power of the poem is perhaps largely due to the emphasis which Whittier throws upon the human side of the picture. Nature meant comparatively little to him, as to most New Englanders. The snow occupies him for a moment, but what really echoes in his memory is not the outward accident of the season, but the picturesque and typical concentration and isolation of the family life of which it was the cause. The weather and the landscape are adequately treated, though without emphasis. There is no pretty description of the winter brook, as in Lowell — it is simply silent. The light converges in turn on each figure in the family group, on his special traits. Nature is subordinated, even at nature's height of power, to human character.

Third, it was an old man, tender-hearted, who thus drew the portraits of the circle of which he and his brother alone survived. The mood was one of wistful and reverential piety — the thoughtful farmer's mood, in many a land, under many a religion, recalling the ancient scenes more clearly as his memory for recent things grows less secure, living with fond regret the departed days, yearning for friends long vanished. Our changed national life, the passing

away of the old agricultural conditions, the
breaking up of ancient traditions, has made this
wistful and reverential mood a constant element
in our recent literature. In poems and novels
we have delighted to reconstruct the past, as the
Arab singers before Mohammed began their lays
with the contemplation of a deserted camping-
ground. It was Whittier that introduced the
new theme, best described in the closing lines of
his own poem : —

> " Yet, haply, in some lull of life,
>   Some Truce of God which breaks its strife,
>   The worldling's eyes shall gather dew,
>   Dreaming in throngful city ways
>   Of winter joys his boyhood knew;
>   And dear and early friends — the few
>   Who yet remain — shall pause to view
>   These Flemish pictures of old days;
>   Sit with me by the homestead hearth,
>   And stretch the hands of memory forth
>   To warm them at the wood-fire's blaze !
>   And thanks untraced to lips unknown
>   Shall greet me like the odors blown
>   From unseen meadows newly mown,
>   Or lilies floating in some pond,
>   Wood-fringed, the wayside gaze beyond;
>   The traveller owns the grateful sense
>   Of sweetness near, he knows not whence,
>   And, pausing, takes with forehead bare
>   The benediction of the air."

In his old age Whittier's heart turned also
with increasing frequency to religious themes,
and we must, last of all, discuss his religious

verse. It must be remembered that in his youth he had been justly called "the gay young Quaker." He was handsome, ambitious, fond of women, with his heart set on political or literary fame. It was only as he neared middle life and had given himself over unselfishly to a humanitarian cause, that his letters and his poems began to show a spirit of religious devotion, which grew deeper and stronger with his advancing years. His religious feeling was not, however, one of creed or convention, but was in this respect typical of a strong minority, existing certainly from early times in his district and probably in all New England. Amesbury had from its foundation been deeply tinged with anti-Puritanical feeling. Indeed, beguiled by the prominence of the local priesthood in affairs and in literature, we often misread the history of New England thought. We may suspect that from the very beginning there was a considerable remnant who had little sympathy with the mechanical creeds and political bigotry of the reigning church. From such a remnant, long without its share in literature, sprang Benjamin Franklin, and we may imagine a continuity of this quietly rebellious remnant — clearheaded, righteous, unsuperstitious, but genuinely religious — through all New England history, standing calmly outside the church or remaining unsympathetic with its doctrine, and forming later the material on which Unitarianism and Universalism drew so largely. Puritanism sat in the seat of power and prominence, but it never was completely victorious. From a thousand hints we may guess the permanence of a brave doubt of that fierce doctrine, combined with a genuine but creedless piety. Many a grizzled Essex County farmer in Whittier's time had pondered long over the sacred books of other religions, had read the Bible with critical care, and was ready to do battle even with the parson himself on the main doctrines of the church, while each respected the honor and purity of the other's life and deeds. In New England, as everywhere among intelligent people, the current state religion was merely the routine form of piety, and Whittier the Quaker, whose religious opinions were independent of books and logic, was no less typical than Cotton Mather or Jonathan Edwards.

We thus find Whittier's attitude toward the various religious movements of his time typical not merely of his own Society but of a strong New England minority. He could not bring himself to conceive of heaven in the old mediæval fashion, " Dante's picture of Heaven, — an old man sitting eternally on a high chair, and concentric circles of saints, martyrs, and ordinary church members whirling around him in perpetual gyration, and singing ' Glory ' ! " [1]   He agreed with " the thoughtful and earnest seekers after truth in other denominations, who find it impossible to accept much which seems to them irreverent and dishonoring to God in creeds founded on an arbitrary arrangement of isolated and often irrelevant texts — the letter that killeth, without the Spirit, which alone gives life.   It is scarcely possible to overestimate the evils of doubt, anguish, despair, and infidelity resulting from doctrines which attribute to the Heavenly Father schemes and designs utterly at variance with the moral sense of his creatures, and which in them would be regarded as unspeakably unjust and cruel." [2]   With Joseph Cook and Mr. Moody, the popular expounders of the old faith in his day, he had little sympathy : —

" I have not read Joseph Cook's letters carefully, but a hasty perusal of two of them gave me the impression of a good deal of ability and smartness on the part of the author.   After all, there is no great use in arguing the question of immortality.   One must feel its truth. You cannot climb into heaven on a syllogism. Moody and Sankey are busy in Boston.   The papers give the discourses of Mr. Moody, which

[1] Pickard, *Life*, ii. 668.
[2] Pickard, *Life*, ii. 723.

seem rather commonplace and poor, but the man
is in earnest, and believes in all the literalness
of the Bible and of John Calvin. I hope he will
do good, and believe that he will reach and
move some who could not be touched by James
Freeman Clarke or Phillips Brooks. I cannot
accept his theology, or part of it at least, and his
methods are not to my taste. But if he can
make the drunkard, the gambler, and the de-
bauchee into decent men, and make the lot of
their weariful wives and children less bitter, I
bid him God-speed." [1]

He even shrank from the Episcopal Church,
which was beginning so deftly to dissolve the old
Unitarian and Congregationalist influences in
Eastern Massachusetts. He wrote to Lucy
Larcom : " I do not wonder that ' the Church '
commends itself to thy mind and heart, so far
as it is represented by Phillips Brooks. But I
am too much of a Quaker to find a home there.
Quakerism has no church of its own — it belongs
to the Church Universal and Invisible." [2]

It was against the intrusion of reason into
religion, against a blind trust in the words of a
book, that Whittier rebelled. His was the Old
Quakerism. " That central doctrine of ours," he
wrote to Professor Gummere of Haverford, —
" the Divine Immanence and Universal Light,

[1] Pickard, *Life*, ii. 628.   [2] *Ibid.* ii. 747.

— will yet be found the stronghold of Christendom, the sure, safe place from superstition on the one hand and scientific doubt on the other."

"We can do without Bible or church," he wrote to Elizabeth Stuart Phelps; "we cannot do without God, and of Him we are sure. All that science and criticism can urge cannot shake the self-evident truth that He asks me to be true, just, merciful, and loving, and because He asks me to be so, I know that He is himself what He requires of me."[1] It was this rigidly simple belief, which scarcely went beyond the statements thus quoted, that made him so typical of all men of deep feeling, and that has placed so many of his poems in the hymnals of several Christian sects. His doctrine was one on which all could unite.

But the inner promptings of the Spirit — independent of book or reason — must seem but a frail support when age presses and friends vanish and the heart cries out for a witness to the hope of a hereafter. Here and there in Whittier's poems we find a trace of the paralyzing fear that the inner sense that tells us of immortality may be but a false gleam of light, and this is particularly true in his letters: —

"As the years pass and one slides so rapidly down the afternoon slope of life, until the dark

[1] Pickard, *Life*, ii. 567.

and chill of the evening shadows rest upon him, he longs for the hands and voices of those who, in the morning, went up on the other side with him. The awful mysteries of life and nature sometimes almost overwhelm me. 'What, Where, Whither?' These questions sometimes hold me breathless. How little, after all, do we know! And the soul's anchor of Faith can only grapple fast upon two or three things, and first and surest of all upon the Fatherhood of God." [1]

It was under the spur of such dread that his thoughts turned often to spiritualism, a belief towards which he had a plain leaning. His acuteness of judgment made him suspect fraud in many alleged manifestations, but he followed carefully the work of the English Society for Psychical Research, whose " investigations are conducted strictly on scientific principles; " he hoped but scarcely expected that " some clue may be found to the great mystery of life and death — and the beyond; " [2] and he craved himself for some sign : —

" 'I have had as good a chance to see a ghost,' he once said, ' as anybody ever had, but not the slightest sign ever came to me. I do not doubt what others tell me, but I sometimes wonder over my own incapacity. I should like to see some dear ghost walk in and sit

[1] Pickard, *Life*, ii. 625.   [2] *Ibid*. ii. 720.

down by me when I am here alone. The doings of the old witch days have never been explained, and as we are so soon to be transferred to another state, how natural it appears that some of us should have glimpses of it here! We all feel the help we receive from the Divine Spirit. Why deny, then, that some men have it more directly and more visibly than others?' " [1]

Not reason, nor research, nor faith could altogether quiet in him the flickering human doubt. *Where, whither, what, how?* are the questions that repeat themselves in his letters, only to be answered by the firm answers of faith. And it is this subordination of doubt, rather than its annihilation, this childlike and manlike trust, that has made his religious poetry so deeply and widely beloved.

The years of this last period of Whittier's life were eventless. He was still an invalid. Headaches oppressed him after any prolonged mental effort, and he was harassed by sleeplessness, and now and then prostrated by severe illnesses. The bitter northern winters had always troubled him, and as his strength failed slowly he shrank from the excessive summer heat. But he habituated himself to the discomforts of age and weakness, managed wisely the strength he had, and lived, all in all, a placid and happy life,

[1] Mrs. Fields, *Whittier*, 35.

interested in local and national affairs, reading
widely in works of travel, history, and pure literature, and happy in the society of his friends
and in the necessary routine of life.

Between Whittier and his younger sister,
Elizabeth, there existed the strongest bonds of
affection, heightened by a somewhat close simi-
larity in their tastes and temperaments. Lucy
Larcom, who knew both well, thus sensitively describes, in her journal, their life together : —

"At Amesbury, — with two of the dearest
friends my life is blessed with, — dear quiet
Lizzie, and her poet brother. I love to sit with
them in the still Quaker worship, and they love
the free air and all the beautiful things as much
as they do all the good and spiritual. The hare-
bells nodding in shade and shine on the steep
banks of the Merrimac, the sparkle of the waters,
the blue of the sky, the balm of the air, and the
atmosphere of grave sweet friendliness which I
breathed for one calm 'First Day' are never to
be forgotten. . . .

"But theirs is a home in each other's love,
which makes earth a place to cling to for its
beauty yet. If I could not think of them together there, of the quiet light which bathes
everything within and around their cottage under
the shadow of the hill, of the care repaid by
gentle trust, and the dependence so blessed in

its shelter of tenderness and strength, the world would seem to me a much drearier place; for I have never seen anything like this brother's and sister's love, and the home atmosphere it creates, the trust in human goodness and the Divine Love it diffuses into all who enter the charmed circle." [1]

After the death of his sister in 1864, he still occupied the pretty little house in Amesbury, which was kept for him by his niece, Elizabeth Whittier. When, in 1876, she married Mr. Samuel T. Pickard, he became for a great part of the years that remained to him the guest of his cousins, the Misses Johnson, at Oak Knoll, a beautiful estate at Danvers, which they had recently purchased; but the Amesbury house was usually kept open for him, so that he might return for shorter or longer intervals. His income from royalties on his books had now for some years largely exceeded his needs, and though he gave much in charity, he was not obliged to write more than he chose nor to take anxious thought about his worldly affairs. From time to time he came to Boston for short periods, either going to the house of an intimate friend or to a quiet hotel. His summers he spent at Amesbury, at Danvers, at the Isles of Shoals with Celia Thaxter, or in company with relatives in pleasant New Hampshire inns on

[1] D. D. Addison, *Lucy Larcom* (1894), 98, 135.

Lake Winnepesaukee or near Chocorua. We may fancy his old age, then, as happy in all these environments. At Amesbury he had lived the old life of the citizen and neighbor, well known and none the less loved, a prophet honored in his own country. He mingled freely with old friends, whom he often met in the shop of a village tailor, himself a man of much acuteness and breadth of mind; he kept in touch with local affairs; he helped many by counsel and by gifts — it was the old country life. At Danvers he was, though so near, yet remote. The high-backed hills shut out the Merrimac valley. He was not familiarly known to the rural folk, though many a lad such as I, hunting for birds' nests in the woods thereabouts, or tramping up and down that Roman-straight Newburyport turnpike, knew that somewhere near lived the gray old country poet. Cut off from the old village life, with its neighbor intimacies, its jostle of interests, its smack of the farm and store and factory, he had here the seclusion of a beautiful estate, with its ways of comfort and distinction; the pleasures of the farm without its toil; orchards, fine trees, and lawns; companionship in life of a more stately fashion. In Boston, on his occasional visits, he was made as much of as he would, and could feel himself the man of national reputation, whom people of wealth and

high social standing were glad to have in their
houses. In New Hampshire, he enjoyed the physical stimulus and mental relaxation which came
from noble scenery, the fresh air of the lake and
the mountains, the restful companionship of relatives and friends, — summer pleasures new to
one who had long spent all the year round, alter-
nately chilled or baked, in the same little house
in a bustling lowland village. From all these
sources came the content of satisfied old age
after a middle life of heart-breaking endeavor,
scanty means, and narrow opportunities.

Whittier's life, however, was at best a lonely
one. An invalid and a bachelor, he was, too,
almost entirely deprived of intimate friendship
with men. His fiery devotion to humanitarian
aims had brought him into close and cordial relations with certain men whom he loved, as with
Sumner, but such friendships were maintained
mostly by correspondence and lacked in a measure the warmth and completeness which he must
have craved. At Amesbury he had frequent
companionship with certain of his neighbors,
and such relations were again eminently characteristic and satisfactory, though mainly due
to the accidents of contiguity. But he was a
thoroughly reticent man, in essence ascetic and
restrained, and whether by force of circumstances or by preference, there was throughout

his life apparently no one man or group of men with whom he was long on terms of complete intimacy, or to whom he was accustomed to open his heart. Sumner he loved and Bayard Taylor, though he saw either but rarely, and he admired Whipple greatly. With Longfellow he had only an acquaintanceship, and between him and Holmes, who in later years wrote to him and of him so warmly, there was little in common except their old age and their poetic fame. Hawthorne he knew scarcely at all, and he sometimes spoke with quaint humor of his sensations in calling on him once when Hawthorne's preoccupied and solemn air made him look to Whittier "as if he had just come up from down cellar." With Emerson he was on better, though not at all intimate, terms, and he was accustomed to relate several characteristic anecdotes of him. In one Emerson remarked that a devout Calvinist prayed for him daily, adding that he himself offered a prayer for himself each day. " Does thee ? " said Whittier. " What does thee pray for, friend Emerson ? " " Well," replied Mr. Emerson, " when I first open my eyes upon the morning meadows, and look out upon the beautiful world, I thank God that I am alive, and that I live so near Boston." [1] But such an incident, though amusing, shows the lack of

[1] Mrs. Claflin, *Personal Recollections of John G. Whittier*, 26.

real depth and community of interest between them.

Foreign visitors often came to see Whittier. He liked Dickens well and recognized Matthew Arnold's virtues; for Charles Kingsley he had a hearty affection. With the brilliant Southern poet, Paul Hamilton Hayne, who visited him at Oak Knoll, he long kept up a friendly correspondence, indicative on both sides of a breadth of mind and heartiness of feeling that augured well for the rapid reconciliation of the North and the South. But his most familiar acquaintances were almost invariably women; and this was natural. Ascetic in life, not touching wine or tobacco, unused to sport, frail of health, isolated in residence, without employment that brought him into regular contact with his fellows, reticent and shy, there was no line of communication open between his life and that of men of robust and active habits, whose peer he really was. Women understood better his prim and gentle ways, his physical delicacy, his saintly devotion to spiritual ideals. His most frequent correspondents were women, — Lucy Larcom, Alice and Phœbe Cary, Celia Thaxter, Gail Hamilton, Mrs. Stowe, Elizabeth Stuart Phelps, Edith Thomas, Sarah Orne Jewett, Edna Dean Proctor, Mrs. Fields, Mrs. Claflin, — and his letters to them show sincere friendship and community of spirit. In old age his was the point of view, the theory of life, of the woman of gentle tastes, literary interests, and religious feeling. The best accounts of his later life are those of Mrs. Claflin and Mrs. Fields, in whose houses he was often a guest; and they have much to say of his sincere friendliness and quiet talk, his shy avoidance of notoriety or even of a large group of people, his keen sense of humor, his tales of his youth, his quaintly serious comments on life, his sudden comings and goings, as inclination moved, and of the rare occasions when, deeply moved, he spoke of the great issues of religion with beautiful earnestness and simple faith. And it is pleasant to think of this farmer's lad, who had lived for forty years in all but poverty for the love of God and his fellows, taking an innocent delight in the luxury of great houses and in the sheltered life of those protected from hardship and privation. After his long warfare this was a just reward.

Thus the years passed, bringing him peace and pleasant associations, and love and honor from the people. His birthdays were celebrated with increasing respect as his age advanced. In 1877, the seventieth anniversary, the " Literary World " of Boston devoted an entire issue to tributes to him in prose and verse from men and women of letters, and he was the guest of

honor at a dinner given by the publishers of the
" Atlantic Monthly " to its distinguished con-
tributors. In 1887 the commonwealth itself
paid him the honor due for his eminence not
only in literature but in politics, the governor
and other distinguished citizens coming to Oak
Knoll to present their congratulations. The
succeeding anniversaries were observed in schools
throughout a large part of the United States.
He had lived to be one of the last representatives of the abolitionist cause and of the old
group of New England poets, and he stood to
the whole nation for antique virtue, for a race
of men now passed away.

In the winter of 1892 he barely rallied from
the terrible " grippe," less a cold than a pesti-
lent scourge of humanity ; but in the following
spring and summer he recovered somewhat his
strength, and proposed spending a little time at
the house of an old friend at Hampton Falls,
N. H. Here, under the colonial elms or on the
balcony on which his room opened, he rested,
looking out over the meadows, watching the distant ships, reading, dreaming of old days, and,
free from the intrusion of strangers, holding
pleasant conversations with dear friends. But
his strength was frail and a slight illness prostrated him ; and death — peaceful and comparatively painless — soon followed. Almost his

last words were " Love — love to all the world."
His funeral services were held in the little garden in Amesbury on which his study opened,
and he was buried in the village cemetery on
the hill that overlooks the valley he loved.
Around him are the graves of his family, for he
was the last survivor of the circle that gathered
about the hearth in the snow-bound homestead.
And, such was his art, there is no other family in the world whose members are so widely
known among the peoples who speak the English
tongue.

In person Whittier was tall, slender, dark of
complexion, and of active habit. At the age
of twenty-seven " he wore a dark frock-coat, with
standing collar, which, with his thin hair, dark
and sometimes flashing eyes, and black whiskers,
not large, but noticeable in those unhirsute days,
gave him, to my then unpractised eye, quite as
much of a military as a Quaker aspect. His
broad square forehead and well-cut features,
aided by his incipient reputation as a poet, made
him quite a noticeable feature of the convention." [1] Mr. Higginson's memory of him at
thirty-five presents the same characteristics more
vividly : " I saw before me a man of striking personal appearance ; tall, slender, with olive com-

[1] J. Miller McKim, quoted in Pickard, *Life*, i. 135.

plexion, black hair, straight, black eyebrows,
brilliant eyes, and an Oriental, Semitic cast of
countenance." [1]   And Mr. Robert S. Rantoul
speaks of him as having "the reticence and
presence of an Arab chief, with the eye of an
eagle." [2]   In later life he was at first sight a less
impressive figure, with a touch of rusticity, and
the dress and bearing of an older time, but always dignified and alert.   Mr. Gosse, who visited
him in 1884, describes accurately his appearance
in old age : —

"Mr. Whittier himself appeared, with all that
report had ever told of gentle sweetness and dignified cordial courtesy.   He was then seventy-
seven years old, and, although he spoke of age
and feebleness, he showed few signs of either;
he was, in fact, to live eight years more. . . .
The peculiarity of his face rested in the extraordinary large and luminous black eyes, set in
black eyebrows, and fringed with thick black
eyelashes curiously curved inwards.   This bar of
vivid black across the countenance was startlingly
contrasted with the bushy snow-white beard and
hair, offering a sort of contradiction which
was surprising and presently pleasing. . . . He
struck me as very gay and cheerful, in spite of

[1] T. W. Higginson, *Whittier* (1902), 94.
[2] *Historical Collections of the Essex Institute*, xxxvii (1901),
135.

his occasional references to the passage of time and the vanishing of beloved faces. He even laughed, frequently and with a childlike sudden-ness, but without a sound. His face had none of the immobility so frequent with very aged persons; on the contrary, waves of mood were always sparkling across his features, and leaving nothing stationary there except the narrow, high, and strangely receding forehead. His language, very fluid and easy, had an agreeable touch of the soil, an occasional rustic note in its elegant colloquialism, that seemed very pleasant and appropriate, as if it linked him naturally with the long line of sturdy ancestors of whom he was the final blossoming. In connection with his poetry, I think it would be difficult to form in the imagination a figure more appropriate to Whittier's writings than Whittier himself proved to be in the flesh." [1]

In the criticism of Whittier's work there re-mains little to be said, even by way of summary. His prose pieces, perhaps, deserve more credit than is usually given them, but they do not show genius. His verse deals, first, with reform; second, with New England life, both historically and in reminiscence; third, with faith in God and immortality. The reforms he advocated

[1] "A Visit to Whittier," *The Bookman*, viii. 459.

were temporary, and his verses of this sort will doubtless be obscured by time. Many have already lost their interest. But their vehemence and elevation of spirit would long preserve a few, even were they not closely associated with the most critical period of our national history. His historical ballads are almost supreme in their class, and his poems memorial of the old farm life are unique; both must live long by the sheer potency of their matter and by the virtue of their simple but delicate art. His religious verse, of less striking merit, is less sure of comparative permanency, but has clearly many chances of survival, due to the author's simple-minded faith in an age preëminently of intellectual doubt.

Adverse criticism of Whittier's verse is mainly confined to three points, — its unequal value, its tendency to moralize, and its loose rhymes. All three points are well taken. Inequality in poetic work, however, does not deeply concern the contemporary reading public or that of posterity. We have only to put aside the trivial and to retain the worthy, thankful for whatever remains after the sifting. A moralizing poet, to touch on the second point for an instant, Whittier certainly was, nor can we imagine him as anything widely different. The reforming element belonged to the essence of his nature; and he was

in this respect profoundly typical of New England. We must frankly accept him as he was.
Whitman, whose point of view was so opposite,
judged him wisely. " Whittier's poetry," he
said in a letter to Mr. Kennedy, " stands for
morality . . . as filtered through the positive
Puritanical and Quaker filters; is very valuable
as a genuine utterance. . . . Whittier is rather
a grand figure — pretty lean and ascetic — no
Greek — also not composite and universal enough
(does n't wish to be, does n't try to be) for ideal
Americanism." [1] Lastly, Whittier's apparently
inaccurate rhymes are sometimes due to his fidel-
ity to the pronunciation with which he was familiar. More frequently, they are due to the fact
that his ear was often pleased, as is mine, by
an approximate rhyme or by a rough assonance.
The critics forget that in this particular the public is largely, and has always been, on his side.
Minute accuracy in rhyme seems to me a somewhat pedantic and bookish notion.

In form his poetic product is characterized by
extreme simplicity, and his skill is due to native
talent, supplemented by much practice under
circumstances that gave him such interest in his
matter that he was scarcely conscious of his
manner. His style was, moreover, repeatedly
modified by the influence of other poets. From

[1] W. S. Kennedy, *Whittier* (American Reformers), 220.

the point of view of form, he achieved his greatest success in the ballad, especially where the tale was one long familiar to him, — so familiar, indeed, that it was remembered and forgotten in turn until it one day took on an almost perfect shape.

Of American poets he appeals, with Longfellow, to the plain people, to the major part of the inhabitants of the land. Both were, in spite of great differences in education and experience, singularly simple-minded men. As a professor Longfellow might have become a pedant. As a reformer Whittier might have become a pessimist or a politician. Both remained almost childlike. Life was to both an infinitely simple matter. Longfellow had the greater breadth of mind; Whittier, the greater intensity. Longfellow had more richness and variety of tone; Whittier, more sincerity. Both were by nature singers, and for the nation at large none of their contemporaries can compare with either.

It might be said that this simplicity, this lack of intellectual breadth and depth, stamps Whittier as a minor English poet. Those of us, however, who hesitate to rank poets according to a conventional system would prefer merely to say that he may properly be classed with poets of simple thought and feeling, rather than with poets of intricate art or intricate feeling or intricate thought, — different from these, then, rather than greater or less. His best analogue is Burns, of whose general type he is. His life was more noble, his verse of much the same importance, I should say, to Americans as that of Burns to Scotchmen. He was so strictly a local poet that it is doubtful of what permanent value he will be to other nations using our common language, but with us his fame is secure.

APPENDIX

I

WHITTIER'S AUTOBIOGRAPHICAL LETTER

[Printed privately, for use in correspondence.]

AMESBURY, 5th Mo., 1882.

DEAR FRIEND, — I am asked in thy note of this morning to give some account of my life. There is very little to give. I can say with Canning's knife-grinder: "Story, God bless you! I have none to tell you!"

I was born on the 17th of December, 1807, in the easterly part of Haverhill, Mass., in the house built by my first American ancestor, two hundred years ago. My father was a farmer, in moderate circumstances, — a man of good natural ability, and sound judgment. For a great many years he was one of the Selectmen of the town, and was often called upon to act as arbitrator in matters at issue between neighbors. My mother was Abigail Hussey, of Rollinsford, N. H. A bachelor uncle and a maiden aunt, both of whom I remember with much affection, lived in the family. The farm was not a very profitable one; it was burdened with debt and we had no spare money; but with strict economy we lived comfortably and respectably. Both my parents were members of the Society of Friends. I had a brother and two sisters.

Our home was somewhat lonely, half hidden in oak woods, with no house in sight, and we had few companions of our age, and few occasions of recreation. Our school was only for twelve weeks in a year, — in the depth of winter, and half a mile distant. At an early age I was set at work on the farm, and doing errands for my mother, who, in addition to her ordinary house duties, was busy in spinning and weaving the linen and woollen cloth needed in the family. On First-days father and mother, and sometimes one of the children, rode down to the Friends' Meeting-house in Amesbury, eight miles distant. I think I rather enjoyed staying at home and wandering in the woods, or climbing Job's hill, which rose abruptly from the brook which rippled down at the foot of our garden. From the top of the hill I could see the blue outline of the Deerfield mountains in New Hampshire, and the solitary peak of Agamenticus on the coast of Maine. A curving line of morning mist marked the course of the Merrimac, and Great Pond, or Kenoza, stretched away from the foot of the hill towards the village of Haverhill, hidden from sight by intervening hills and woods, but which sent to us the sound of its two church bells. We had only about twenty volumes of books, most of them the journals of pioneer ministers in our society. Our only annual was an almanac. I was early fond of reading, and now and then heard of a book of biography or travel, and walked miles to borrow it.

When I was fourteen years old my first schoolmaster, Joshua Coffin, the able, eccentric historian of

Newbury, brought with him to our house a volume
of Burns's poems, from which he read, greatly to my
delight. I begged him to leave the book with me,
and set myself at once to the task of mastering the
glossary of the Scottish dialect at its close. This was
about the first poetry I had ever read (with the exception of that of the Bible, of which I had been a close
student), and it had a lasting influence upon me. I
began to make rhymes myself, and to imagine stories
and adventures. In fact I lived a sort of dual life, and
in a world of fancy, as well as in the world of plain
matter-of-fact about me. My father always had a
weekly newspaper, and when young Garrison started
his "Free Press" at Newburyport, he took it in the
place of the "Haverhill Gazette." My sister, who
was two years older than myself, sent one of my
poetical attempts to the editor. Some weeks afterwards the news-carrier came along on horseback and
threw the paper out from his saddle-bags. My uncle
and I were mending fences. I took up the sheet,
and was surprised and overjoyed to see my lines in
the "Poet's Corner." I stood gazing at them in wonder, and my uncle had to call me several times to
my work before I could recover myself. Soon after,
Garrison came to our farmhouse, and I was called
in from hoeing in the corn-field to see him. He
encouraged me, and urged my father to send me
to school. I longed for education, but the means to
procure it were wanting. Luckily, the young man
who worked for us on the farm in summer, eked out
his small income by making ladies' shoes and slippers

in the winter; and I learned enough of him to earn
a sum sufficient to carry me through a term of six
months in the Haverhill Academy. The next winter
I ventured upon another expedient for raising money,
and kept a district school in the adjoining town of
Amesbury, thereby enabling me to have another
academy term. The next winter I spent in Boston,
writing for a paper. Returning in the spring, while
at work on the farm, I was surprised by an invitation to take charge of the Hartford (Ct.) "Review,"
in the place of the famous George D. Prentice, who
had removed to Kentucky. I had sent him some
of my school "compositions," which he had received
favorably. I was unwilling to lose the chance of
doing something more in accordance with my taste,
and, though I felt my unfitness for the place, I accepted it, and remained nearly two years, when I was
called home by the illness of my father, who died
soon after. I then took charge of the farm, and
worked hard to "make both ends meet;" and, aided
by my mother's and sister's thrift and economy, in
some measure succeeded.

As a member of the Society of Friends, I had been
educated to regard Slavery as a great and dangerous evil, and my sympathies were strongly enlisted
for the oppressed slaves by my intimate acquaintance
with William Lloyd Garrison. When the latter
started his paper in Vermont, in 1828, I wrote him
a letter commending his views upon Slavery, Intemperance and War, and assuring him that he was destined to do great things. In 1833 I was a delegate

to the first National Anti-Slavery Convention, at Philadelphia. I was one of the Secretaries of the Convention and signed its Declaration. In 1835 I was in the Massachusetts Legislature. I was mobbed in Concord, N. H., in company with George Thompson, afterwards member of the British Parliament, and narrowly escaped from great danger. I kept Thompson, whose life was hunted for, concealed in our lonely farmhouse for two weeks. I was in Boston during the great mob in Washington Street, soon after, and was threatened with personal violence. In 1837 I was in New York, in conjunction with Henry B. Stanton and Theodore D. Weld, in the office of the American Anti-Slavery Society. The next year I took charge of the "Pennsylvania Freeman," an organ of the Anti-Slavery Society. My office was sacked and burned by a mob soon after, but I continued my paper until my health failed, when I returned to Massachusetts. The farm in Haverhill had, in the mean time, been sold, and my mother, aunt, and youngest sister had moved to Amesbury, near the Friends' Meeting-house, and I took up my residence with them. All this time I had been actively engaged in writing for the anti-slavery cause. In 1833 I printed at my own expense an edition of my first pamphlet, "Justice and Expediency." With the exception of a few dollars from the "Democratic Review" and "Buckingham's Magazine," I received nothing for my poems and literary articles. Indeed, my pronounced views on Slavery made my name too unpopular for a publisher's uses. I edited in 1844

" The Middlesex Standard," and afterwards became associate editor of the " National Era," at Washington. I early saw the necessity of separate political action on the part of abolitionists ; and was one of the founders of the Liberty party — the germ of the present Republican party.

In 1857 an edition of my complete poems, up to that time, was published by Ticknor & Fields. " In War Times " followed in 1864, and in 1865 " Snow-Bound." In 1860 I was chosen a member of the Electoral College of Massachusetts, and also in 1864. I have been a member of the Board of Overseers of Harvard College, and a Trustee of Brown University. But while feeling, and willing to meet all the responsibilities of citizenship, and deeply interested in questions which concern the welfare and honor of the country, I have, as a rule, declined overtures for acceptance of public stations. I have always taken an active part in elections, but have not been willing to add my own example to the greed of office.

I have been a member of the Society of Friends by birthright, and by a settled conviction of the truth of its principles and the importance of its testimonies, while, at the same time, I have a kind feeling towards all who are seeking, in different ways from mine, to serve God and benefit their fellow-men.

Neither of my sisters are living. My dear mother, to whom I owe much every way, died in 1858. My brother is still living, in the city of Boston. My niece, his daughter, who was with me for some years, is now the wife of S. T. Pickard, Esq., of Portland,

Maine. Since she left me I have spent much of my time with esteemed relatives at Oak Knoll, Danvers, Mass., though I still keep my homestead at Amesbury, where I am a voter.

My health was never robust; I inherited from both my parents a sensitive, nervous temperament; and one of my earliest recollections is of pain in the head, from which I have suffered all my life. For many years I have not been able to read or write for more than half an hour at a time; often not so long. Of late, my hearing has been defective. But in many ways I have been blest far beyond my deserving; and, grateful to the Divine Providence, I tranquilly await the close of a life which has been longer, and on the whole happier, than I had reason to expect, although far different from that which I dreamed of in youth. My experience confirms the words of old time, that "it is not in man who walketh to direct his steps." Claiming no exemption from the sins and follies of our common humanity, I dare not complain of their inevitable penalties. I have had to learn renunciation and submission, and

> "Knowing
> That kindly Providence its care is showing
> In the withdrawal as in the bestowing,
> Scarcely I dare for more or less to pray."

Thy friend,

JOHN G. WHITTIER.

LIST OF WHITTIER'S WRITINGS

[Separate editions of single short poems are omitted, as well as the successive editions, after 1849, of his *Poems*. Full bibliographical material will be found in Foley's *American Authors* and in Bierstadt's " Bibliography of Whittier " in the *Book Buyer* for 1896.]

Legends of New England. Hartford, 1831.

The Literary Remains of John G. C. Brainard, with a Sketch of his Life. Hartford, 1832.

[Anonymous.] Moll Pitcher, a Poem. Boston, 1832.

Justice and Expediency ; or Slavery considered with a View to its Rightful and Effectual Remedy, Abolition. Haverhill, 1833.

Mogg Megone, a Poem. Boston, 1836.

Views of Slavery and Emancipation ; from Society in America. By Harriet Martineau. (With an Introduction by Whittier.) New York, 1837.

Letters from John Quincy Adams to his Constituents of the Twelfth Congressional District in Massachusetts. (With Introductory Remarks by Whittier.) Boston, 1837.

Poems written during the Progress of the Abolition Question in the United States, between the Years 1830 and 1838. Boston, 1837.

[Anonymous.] Narrative of James Williams, an

American Slave, who was for Several Years a Driver on a Cotton Plantation in Alabama. New York, 1838.

Poems. Philadelphia, 1838.

Moll Pitcher and The Minstrel Girl. Poems. Revised Edition. Philadelphia, 1840.

Lays of my Home and Other Poems. Boston, 1843.

[Anonymous.] The Stranger in Lowell. Boston, 1845.

Voices of Freedom. Philadelphia, 1846.

The Supernaturalism of New England. By the author of The Stranger in Lowell. New York, 1847.

[Anonymous.] Leaves from Margaret Smith's Journal in the Province of Massachusetts Bay. 1678–79. Boston, 1849.

Poems. Boston, 1849.

Old Portraits and Modern Sketches. Boston, 1850.

Songs of Labor and Other Poems. Boston, 1850.

The Chapel of the Hermits and Other Poems. Boston, 1853.

Literary Recreations and Miscellanies. Boston, 1854.

The Panorama and Other Poems. Boston, 1856.

Home Ballads and Poems. Boston, 1860.

The Patience of Hope. By the author of " A Present Heaven " (Dora Greenwell). (With an Introduction by Whittier.) Boston, 1862.

In War Time and Other Poems. Boston, 1864.

National Lyrics. Boston, 1865.

Snow-Bound. A Winter Idyl. Boston, 1866.

The Tent on the Beach and Other Poems. Boston, 1867.

Among the Hills and Other Poems. Boston, 1869.

Ballads of New England. Boston, 1870.

Two Letters on the Present Aspect of the Society of Friends. London, 1870.

Miriam and Other Poems. Boston, 1871.

The Journal of John Woolman. (With an Introduction by Whittier.) Boston, 1871.

The Pennsylvania Pilgrim and Other Poems. Boston, 1872.

[Edited.] Child Life : a Collection of Poems. Boston, 1872.

[Edited.] Child Life in Prose. Boston, 1874.

Hazel-Blossoms. Boston, 1875.

Mabel Martin. A Harvest Idyl. Boston, 1876.

[Edited.] Songs of Three Centuries. Boston, 1876.

Indian Civilization : a Lecture by Stanley Pumphrey. (With an Introduction by Whittier.) Philadelphia, 1877.

The Vision of Echard and Other Poems. Boston, 1878.

William Lloyd Garrison and his Times. By Oliver Johnson. (With an Introduction by Whittier.) Boston, 1880.

The King's Missive and Other Poems. Boston, 1881.

Letters of Lydia Maria Child. (With a Biographical Introduction by Whittier.) Boston, 1882.

The Bay of Seven Islands and Other Poems. Boston, 1883.

Saint Gregory's Guest and Recent Poems. Boston, 1886.

Writings (newly revised).   Boston, 1888–89.
At Sundown.   Boston, 1892.
Complete Poetical Works (including all poems col-
lected since the author's death).   Boston, 1895.

INDEX

Abolition movement, its relation to other reforms, 103 ; causes, 107 ; Garrison and the "Liberator," 11; Whittier joins the movement, 120 ; founding of the American Anti-Slavery Society, 125 ; rapid growth, 129 ; divisions in the ranks, 131 ; the new organization, 135; continued growth, 184 ; beginnings of an anti-slavery party, 186; differences of opinion as to political action, 187 ; triumph of the cause, 255.

Adams, J.Q., 149, 158, 164.

American Anti-Slavery Society, 125, 134, 135, 162, 164, 256.

American and Foreign Anti-Slavery Society, 176, 210.

" American and Foreign Anti-Slavery Reporter," 210.

" American Manufacturer," 54.

" Among the Hills," 268.

" Amy Wentworth," 268.

" Annie and Rhoda," 267.

Arnold, Matthew, 267, 286.

" Barbara Frietchie," 262.

" Barefoot Boy, The," 235.

Beecher, H. W., 253.

" Benedicite," 234.

Birney, J. G., 142.

Bradburn, George, 204.

Brainard, J. G. C., 84.

Browning, Robert, 232, 238, 267.

Bryant, W. C., 1, 2, 4, 43, 93, 225.

Burns, Robert, 30, 34.

Byron, Lord, 49, 94.

" Cassandra Southwick," 236.

Channing, W. E., 131.

" Chapel of the Hermits, The," 230.

Chapman, Mrs. M. W., 132, 199.

Child, Mrs. L. M., 115, 122, 132, 199.

Claflin, Mrs. M. B., 286.

Clay, Henry, 57, 62, 63, 69, 77, 119, 153, 215.

Coffin, Joshua, 30, 128.

Coleridge, S. T., 94.

Cushing, Caleb, 74, 120, 148, 202.

" Demon Lover, The," 94.

Dinsmore, Robert, 31, 246.

" Double-headed Snake of Newbury, The," 236.

" Ein feste Burg ist unser Gott," 260.

" Emancipator, The," 142, 210.

Emerson, R. W., 2, 42, 93, 131, 194, 213, 225, 226, 247, 252, 285.

" Essex Transcript, The," 217.

Everett, Edward, 163, 211.

" Exiles, The," 236.

" Expostulation," 169.

Fields, J. T., 251.

Fields, Mrs. Annie, 286.

" Fire Ship, The," 94.

" From Perugia," 232.

" Gamester, The," 80.

Garrison, W. L., 20, 36–40, 43, 50, 53, 54, 58, 64, 84, 111–122, 126, 130, 132–134, 166, 177, 184, 187–190, 194, 196, 197–199, 210, 214, 255, 256.

" Garrison of Cape Ann, The," 236.

Gay, S. H., 201.

" Gazette," The Haverhill, 40, 43, 45, 47, 59, 60, 62, 75, 83, 119, 125, 163, 166.

Gibbons, Mrs. A. H., 199.

" Grace Greenwood," 250.

" Great Ipswich Fright, The," 247.

Grimké, Angelina E., 146, 196.

Hale, J. P., 206.

Harriman, Edwin, 75.

Hawthorne, Nathaniel, 2, 3, 82, 93, 131, 225, 248, 252, 285.

Hayne, P. H., 286.

Hemans, Mrs. F. D., 43, 99.

" Henchman, The," 269.

" Henry St. Clair," 80.

Higginson, T. W., 194.

"History of Haverhill," 83.
Holmes, O. W., 3, 17, 42, 225, 249, 252, 286.
Hooper, Lucy, 148.
"Hunters of Men," The, 168.
Hutchinson, the, singers, 260.

"Ichabod," 220.
Irving, Washington, 81.

"Justice and Expediency," 120.

Lamson, Stephen, 217.
Larcom, Lucy, 242, 271, 277, 281.
Law, Jonathan, 69, 73.
"Lays of My Home," 230.
"Legends of New England," 81, 99.
"Leaves from Margaret Smith's Journal," 240, 244.
Leavitt, Joshua, 210.
"Liberator, The," 113, 163, 166, 167, 196–198, 210.
"Literary Recreations and Miscellanies," 240, 247.
Lloyd, Elizabeth, jr., 147.
Longfellow, H. W., 3, 4, 17, 42, 93, 102, 131, 166, 225, 247, 248, 252, 265, 266, 285.
Lowell, J. R., 3, 4, 17, 42, 93, 131, 201, 221, 225, 229, 236, 238, 247, 252, 262, 272.

"Mabel Martin," 236.
"Maids of Attitash, The," 268.
Martineau, Harriet, 107, 164.
"Mary Garvin," 236.
Massachusetts Abolition Society, 135.
"Massachusetts Abolitionist, The," 135.
Massachusetts Anti-Slavery Society, 160, 162, 189.
"Massachusetts to Virginia," 18, 220, 222.
"Maud Muller," 237.
"Memories," 234.
"Middlesex Standard, The," 175, 213, 240.
"Minstrel Girl, The," 98.
Mirick, B. L., 84.
"Mogg Megone," 170.
"Moll Pitcher," 98.
Moore, Thomas, 36, 43.
Mott, Richard, 181.
"My Playmate," 269.

"Narrative of James Williams," 165.
"National Anti-Slavery Standard," 227, 229.
"National Era," 176, 240, 246, 247.

"Nervous Man, The," 79.
New England Anti-Slavery Society, 114, 134, 142.
"New England Magazine," 79, 81.
"New England Review," 60, 62, 115.
"New England Superstitions," 87.
"New Year, The," 169.

"Old Portraits and Modern Sketches," 240, 246.
"Opium Eater, The," 80.

"Panorama, The," 230.
Pennsylvania Anti-Slavery Society, 165, 167.
"Pennsylvania Freeman," 142, 165, 166, 198, 227.
"Pennsylvania Pilgrim, The," 266.
"Philanthropist, The (Boston)," 50, 53, 54, 80.
Phillips, Wendell, 132, 163, 188, 253.
Pickard, S. T., 84, 150, 282.
Poe, E. A., 93, 102.
"Poems," 167.
"Poems of Adrian," 47.
"Poems written during the Progress of the Abolition Question," 167.
Prentice, G. D., 60, 62, 96.
"Prophecy of Samuel Sewall, The," 236.

Quincy, Edmund, 132.

Rogers, N. P., 139, 199, 246.
Russ, Cornelia, 66.

Scott, Sir Walter, 98, 170.
"Sea Dream, A," 269.
Sewall, S. E., 191.
Sigourney, Mrs. L. H., 66, 71, 73, 81, 91, 100.
"Skipper Ireson's Ride," 237.
"Slave Ships, The," 168.
Smith, Gerrit, 133.
Snelling, Joseph, 96.
"Snow-Bound," 270.
"Song of the Vermonters, The," 18, 49, 100.
Stanton, H. B., 133, 135, 150.
"Star of Bethlehem, The," 100.
"Stranger in Lowell, The," 240, 247.
Sturge, Joseph, 174, 191, 206, 211.
Sumner, Charles, 186, 192, 194, 206, 207, 252, 253, 257–259, 285.
"Supernaturalism in New England," 240, 242, 247.
"Swan Song of Parson Avery, The," 236.

Tappan, Lewis, 124.
Taylor, Bayard, 248, 253, 285.
" Telling the Bees," 237.
Tennyson, Alfred, 238, 267.
" Texas," 191.
Thayer, A. W., 31, 40, 45–47, 50, 75, 76.
Thompson, George, 130, 139.
Thoreau, H. D., 15, 42, 194.
" Thy Will be Done," 260.
" To my Old Schoolmaster," 235.

" Vaudois Teacher, The," 100, 168.
" Views of Slavery and Emancipation," 164.
" Voices of Freedom," 230.

Webster, Daniel, 10, 220.
Weld, T. D., 142, 146.
Whipple, E. P., 285.
Whitman, Walt, 262.
Whittier, Elizabeth H., 9, 262.
Whittier, John G., birth, 1; characteristic New England product, 2; ancestry, 4; environment of his boyhood, 11; the homestead, 12; farming life, 16; principles absorbed in boyhood, 17; farm work, 25; early education, 26; visit to Boston, 27; reading, 28; introduction to Burns, 30; influence of Burns, 34; first verses, 34; slipper-making, 40; attends Haverhill Academy, 41; youthful verses, 42; increasing reputation, 46; "Poems of Adrian," 47; Byronic verses, 48; first good verses, 49; choosing a vocation, 50; entering the world, 53; editor of the " American Manufacturer," 54; leisure in Boston, 58; returned to Haverhill, 59; edited Haverhill " Gazette," 59; acquaintance with George D. Prentice, 60; edits " New England Review," 62; attitude toward reform, 64; returned to Haverhill, 65; associations in Hartford, 65; illness and despondency, 69; political ambitions, 74; experiments in prose and verse, 78; reflective sketches, 79; moral tales, 80; sentimental tales and tales of wonder, 81; "Legends of New England," 81; Mirick's " History of Haverhill," 83; introduction to edition of Brainard's poems, 84; " New England Superstitions," 87; development of his verse, 88; his literary ambition typical, 88; poems written under the influence of Byron, 94; of Scott and Mrs. Hemans, 99; natural leaning toward abolitionism, 115; renewed relations with Garrison, 116; joins the abolition movement, 120; " Justice and Expediency," 122; shared in the founding of the American Anti-Slavery Society, 125; his description of the convention, 126; the " new organization," 133; devotion to the cause, 136; member of the Legislature, 139; aids George Thompson, 139; edited Haverhill " Gazette," 142; in New York as a secretary of the American Anti-Slavery Society, 142; edited " Pennsylvania Freeman," 142; forced by illness to return home, 143; moved to Amesbury, 144; personal relations with reformers, 144; services to the cause as a politician, 148; as a journalist, 163; as a poet, 166; " Mogg Megone," 170; ill health, 174; poverty, 176; other limitations, 177; his self-centred mind, 179; his religious faith, 180; his devotion to this cause, 183; temporary desire for disunion, 190; worked for the building up of an anti-slavery party, 191; differences of opinion among the abolitionists and Whittier's position, 195; services for abolition through the third party, 202; services as a journalist, 210; as a poet, 219; generally regarded only as an abolitionist poet, 228; lines of development of his verse, 230; his prose, 239; pressure of poverty relaxed, 251; his few intimate friends, 252; decreasing part in politics, 257; his war poems, 259; late narrative poems, 265; of reminiscence, 268; religious, 273; last years, 280; death, 288; his personality, 289; criticism, 291.
Willis, N. P., 59, 93, 102.
Wilson, Henry, 206.
Wright, Elizur, 122, 127, 133, 136, 142.

" Yankee Girl, The," 168.

𝕿𝖍𝖊 𝕽𝖎𝖛𝖊𝖗𝖘𝖎𝖉𝖊 𝕻𝖗𝖊𝖘𝖘

Electrotyped and printed by H. O. Houghton & Co.
Cambridge, Mass., U. S. A.

A LIST OF THE WORKS

OF

John Greenleaf Whittier

Writings of

JOHN GREENLEAF WHITTIER

NO edition of the Poetical and Prose Writings of John Greenleaf Whittier is complete and authorized which does not bear the imprint of Houghton, Mifflin & Company.

COMPLETE WORKS

Riverside Edition. In 7 volumes.

POETRY

1. Narrative and Legendary Poems.
2. Poems of Nature; Poems Subjective and Reminiscent; Religious Poems.
3. Anti-Slavery; Songs of Labor and Reform.
4. Personal Poems; Occasional Poems; Tent on the Beach; Appendix.

PROSE

1. Margaret Smith's Journal; Tales and Sketches.
2. Old Portraits and Modern Sketches; Personal Sketches and Tributes; Historical Papers.
3. The Conflict with Slavery; Politics and Reform; The Inner Life; Criticism.

Each volume, crown 8vo, gilt top; the set, $10.50. With "Life of Whittier" (2 vols.) by SAMUEL T. PICKARD, 9 vols., $14.50.

PROSE WORKS

Riverside Edition. With Notes by the Author, and etched Portrait. 3 vols. crown 8vo, gilt top, $4.50.

POEMS

Riverside Edition. With Portraits, Notes, etc. 4 vols., crown 8vo, gilt top, $6.00.

Handy-Volume Edition. With Portraits, and a View of Whittier's Oak Knoll Home. 4 vols., 16mo, gilt top, in cloth box, $5.00. Bound in full, flexible leather, $8.00.

Cambridge Edition. With a Biographical Sketch, Notes, Index to Titles and First Lines, a Portrait, and an engraving of Whittier's Amesbury Home. Large crown 8vo, gilt top, $2.00.

Library Edition. With Portrait and 15 full-page Photogravures. 8vo, gilt top, $2.50.

Household Edition. With Portrait and Illustrations. Crown 8vo, $1.50.

Cabinet Edition. From new plates, with numbered lines, and Portrait. 16mo, gilt top, $1.00.

SEPARATE POEMS

Snow-Bound. A Winter Idyl. *Holiday Edition.* With eight Photogravures and Portrait. 16mo, gilt top, $1.50.

The Tent on the Beach. *Holiday Edition.* With rubricated Initials and 12 full-page Photogravure Illustrations by CHARLES H. WOODBURY and MARCIA O. WOODBURY. 12mo, gilt top, $1.50.

At Sundown. With Portrait and 8 Photogravures. 16mo, gilt top, $1.50.

Legends and Lyrics. 16mo, gilt top, 75 cents.

COMPILATIONS

Birthday Book. With Portrait and 12 Illustrations. 18mo, $1.00.

Calendar Book. 32mo, parchment-paper, 25 cents.

Year Book. With Portrait. 18mo, $1.00.

Text and Verse. For Every Day in the Year. Scripture Passages and Parallel Selections from WHITTIER's Writings. 32mo, 75 cents.

EDITED BY MR. WHITTIER

Songs of Three Centuries. *Library Edition.* With 40 full-page Illustrations. 8vo, gilt top, $2.50.

Household Edition. Much enlarged. Crown 8vo, $1.50.

Child-Life. A Collection of Poems for and about Children. Finely Illustrated. Crown 8vo, gilt top, $2.00.

Child-Life in Prose. A Volume of Stories, Fancies, and Memories of Child-Life. Finely Illustrated Crown 8vo, gilt top, $2.00.

Many of the above editions may be had in leather bindings of various styles.

HOUGHTON, MIFFLIN & COMPANY

4 Park Street, Boston.   85 Fifth Ave., New York